AF528129

Aqua Environmental Economics

N. Rajalakshmi

SERIALS PUBLICATIONS
NEW DELHI (INDIA)

© N. Rajalakshmi

First Published – 2009

ISBN: 978-81-8387-296-6

All rights reserved with the Publisher, including the right to translate or reproduce this book or parts there of except for brief quotations in critical articles or reviews.

Published by

SERIALS PUBLICATIONS
4800/24, 1st Floor, Ansari Road
Darya Ganj, New Delhi-110002 (India)
Phone : 23245225. Fax : 91-11-23272135
E-mail: serials@satyam.net.in

CONTENTS

PREFACE

This book has essentially the modest aim of introducing what the author believe the concerns and practices of Aqua Environmental Economics. The subject of the book is biological environmental economics or economic interpretation of biological environmental problems still narrowing down to aquatic resources. Economics is still a dismal science though not for the original Malthusian reasons. Economic analysis of biological resources is exceedingly controversial and scarce both in academia and policy frame works. Non economists and biological environmentalists who know little about welfare economics and concepts often think economics as mainly theory built on unrealistic assumptions. This book is intended for a wide range of audience, marine biologists, environmentalists, policy maker's fishery economists and researchers.

Fish stocks are living capital which when combined with other capable of producing food and recreational experiences on a potentially continuing basis. Using a standard welfare economics approach, economically efficient utilization of fish stocks requires obtaining the time path of harvests that will maximize the net present value of production taking into account the full opportunity cost of all inputs involved for bio-resource management purposes it is imperative that the focus on the time path of harvest does not detract from the necessity of using efficient resource combinations. It is more demanding because the production functions and population dynamics are stochastic subject to complete specification. It is highly unlikely that the optimal time path question will be solved in aquaculture. Profit maximising participants with easy entry and operating decisions based on private returns are supposed to have a impact on the property rights and the resource stock. If left unregulated the time path of open access use will result in stock sizes which are too low in terms of production and marginal productivity effect on harvest. From a strict economic efficiency point of view, the goal of management is to find the time path of harvest and input usage. A great deal of theoretical and applied work on bio-economics focusses attention on developing programmes which will achieve biological goals of management without causing inefficient use of resources.

Gordon describes the inefficiency of open access utilization in terms of average and marginal returns to a fishery. The preliminary works relating to fishery economics done by Gordon, Scott and Schaefer provide a good description of the basic insights that are fundamental to the field of biological economics, especially the problem of open access inefficiencies. The standard sustainable revenue and cost curve analysis, which is frequently associated with Gordon and is often used to describe the static operation of a fishery.

Economists have developed sophisticated empirical techniques to elucidate the monetary estimates of environmental values. The global concern in environmental matters in the past stems from the mounting pressure of population explosion and increased demand on the planets natural resources base. The sustainability of environmental assets in these lines of developing countries discussed, require environmental protection integrated with economic policies. Environmental evaluation matching with the eco-friendly economic advancement is the determinant to protect the beautiful and defiled world for another generation. Accounting the natural resources for the future and the present is the burden of environmental economists. The total economic value of environmental goods and services is the sum of use-values and non-use values. The use-value comprises the goods and services to producers and consumers who use or enjoy environmental resources such as water, land, trees, landscapes and air. These values may include the option of using a resource sometime in future.

In bringing out this book discussions with Dr. Yadava, Dr. M. Sakthivel, Dr. Nair, were of high utility. Further, the World Bank supported project was also a source to go in depth in dealing with the subject. Dr. P.V. Dehadrai was also instumental to bring out this publication. I greatly appreciate and acknowledge the discussions with Dr. Parikh and Dr. Jyothi Parikh which has helped a lot. Hope this work will be a piece added to the area of environment and bio-economics. In future, as the authors pre-suppose there is a likelihood of emerging research on this field.

N. Rajalakshmi

1

INTRODUCTION TO AQUA-ECONOMICS

Aquaculture is the farming of water area, like farming land for agricultural products, in order to rear selected species of aquatic plants or animals for human utilisation. The medium of aqua-culture can be fresh water, brackish water of marine environment, depending upon the species to be cultured.

India posseses abundant marine and inland fishery resources with a coast line of over 8219 K.M. in length and vast stretches of fresh and brackish water land i.e., boundless expanse of bays, backwaters and open seas, the extensive estuaries or river mouths, lagoons and mangrove swamps. These extensive water bodies and eco systems associated with suitable food webs are two major pre-requisites for successful aquaculture. In India, there is plenty of scope for aquaculture either be it inland or marine which is mainly due to the physiography of the land, its impounded water bodies and its rivers, the presence of large number of estuaries and back waters, mangrove swamps, the extensive seas surrounding the peninsular India and the islands associated with lagoons and coral reefs. These are not only areas of aqua farming but are also areas of production of seeds, otherwise nurseries, that are required for farming. With this wide diversity of geographical and climatic conditions, different dimensions are formed for the development of a multi-billion dollar aquaculture industry in our country. In the southern maritime states Goa, Karnataka, Kerala, Tamil Nadu, Orissa and Andhra Pradesh are the places were prawns are commercially cultivated.

Traditionally prawn farming is being carried out in West Bengal, Kerala, Karnataka and Goa. Under this system, after the paddy harvest, during the incoming tides prawns are harvested at frequent intervals. In Tamil Nadu total area of an estimated brackish water resource is of 0.08 million hectare and about 27,000 ha. are available for immediate utilisation in the state. Out of the 56,000 ha. of brackish water, 500 ha. is estimated to be under farming. In Kerala out of 65,000 ha. of brackish water, more than 13,000 ha is under the traditional paddy-cum-prawn cultivation system. In Andhra Pradesh the total estimated brackish area of the state is 0.2 million ha. Out of the total area, the estimated area for brackish water farming is found to be about 17,000 ha, out of which 117 ha. area lies under private sector and about 255 ha, lies under public sector. Of all the coastal regions of India, Andhra Pradesh and Tamil Nadu are found suitable for growing shrimps, and a lucarative aquaculture industry has developed in these states in the recent decades.

The world shrimp farming production has increased rapidly for more than a decade but the rate of increase has remained fairly constant. However, in India it has recorded a dramatic increase emerging as the third largest producer of aquaculture shrimp in the world. In 1991, shrimp production accounted for approximately 12 to 14% of the total yield from the fisheries of the world, and is currently the only worldwide growth sector within fisheries (Aqua International, 1995).

More than 50% of this shrimp production in India as well as the world originates from the brackish and marine environment, especially from the coastal zone. In fact, coastal shrimp produces more than 90% of the molluscs, crustaceans and seaweeds in the world harvest and roughly 95% of this was produced by only 20 nations located mainly in tropical Asia. The total world shrimp production is expected to reach 22 million metric tonnes by the turn of the century, and a substantial proportion of this would continue to be produced in the marine coastal zone. However, the dramatic expansion of the industry in India has introduced new concerns, especially in terms of environmental degradation.

Shrimp culture industry is taking roots in India. There is perceived need to develop an 'appropriate' shrimp aquaculture technology to enable India emerge as a long-term sustainable source of shrimp, and not go through the boom burst cycle commonly associated with this industry. India has some differences when compared to other S.E. Asian Countries such as : abundant land and labour, supply varying climatic zones, weak infrastructure and paucity of power supply. It is because of these that the farming techniques adapted in India will be different from those used in other countries and will also differ from region to region. For instance, in high saline areas like Ramnad, Tuticorin, Sirkali and certain parts of Thanjavur and Chidambaram of Tamil Nadu State, particularly during Feb/ March crops, farmers can as well try *Penaeus indicus* (K.B. Pillai, 1995).

But sometimes due to the human greed to grab the benefits instantly in many places, farmers are destroying the environment. Prawn farmers should keep in their minds that aquaculture systems are an integrate part of the environment and due consideration must be given to their environmental impact. It is extremely important that the environmental issues be dealt with, since in many instances ecological changes can become risk factors to the industry itself.

The expansion has led to growing concern about environmental issues related to both the impacts of shrimp culture on the environment and impacts of surrounding environment (e.g. via pollution) on shrimp culture. Environmental impacts to the shrimp farm have been often linked to major outbreaks of shrimp disease, production crashes, loss or degradation of natural resources and conflicts with other coastal resource users. All of these appear to be threatening the long-term sustainability of what has undoubtedly become a world's fastest growing aquaculture industry. A major goal of society should be to stimulate production and consumption that do not diminish the capacity of life-support systems to recover after disturbance and that remains within the carrying capacity of the supporting eco-systems. To develop eco-friendly coastal shrimp farming in India, it is desirable to follow extensive method with low stocking density in the areas where the environmental conditions are not stable and semi-intensive method in the areas where conditions are conducive for shrimps and other fishes to grow. The stocking density should vary according to the local salinity conditions and other ecological parameters. In the state of Andhra Pradesh and Tamil Nadu, there are many areas located in the seafront with facilities to draw sea water directly. They are in a position to practice semi-intensive shrimp farming with a stocking density of 20-25/m^2 in the case of tiger shrimp and 25-30/m^2 in the case of white shrimp. This will allow the carrying capacity of the environment longer.

Abstraction of the freshwater from underground aquifers and release of saline water due to semi intensive shrimp farming in different countries have resulted in salt water intrusion and salinisation of freshwater aquifers. This has resulted in the degradation of potable and agriculture water supplies. The problem seems to be particularly acute in areas where shrimp culture is sited inland, and the situation may be made worse by evaporation in the ponds. In many of the coastal areas of Asia, freshwater supplies are scarce and deliberate salinisation and utilisation for shrimp culture seems hardly justified in either social or economic term.

A large area with varying environmental conditions are available along the creeks and estuaries. In West Bengal alone, the high tide sea water floods a large area of the Gangetic delta with varying salinity from the seaface. Similar conditions prevail in other major river systems, estuaries and creeks. During rainy months, the salinity drops to zero and shoots up in summer months. Many rivers and creeks have high or hyper saline water, especially during summer/dry months when the bar mouth is closed. There is hardly any water exchange or influx of any freshwater. As a result, the water conditions are not conducive for shrimps to grow.

Though the development of Aquaculture industry along the coastal regions of Tamil Nadu and Andhra Pradesh appears a big boom owing to a tremendous increase in the export earning of the country environmental degradation due to pollutants from the aquaculture industry has been recognised to be devastating by the environmentalists. This has further led to the depletion of the coastal fishery resources and has declined the sustainable yield of the fishery products. Proper management of the disposal of the aquaculture wastes into the sea has not been regulated for the sustainable development of the fishery stock. Introduction of the aqua wastes and the effluents through biofilters can be recycled for the cultivation of the other species like tilapia that can further enhance the production of farmed products. If not, the treated wastes can be introduced to the coastal environment since it does not cause any deleterious effects in the coastal environment.

TAMIL NADU

The area of the state is 1,30,069 sq.km. It is the 11th biggest state in India that ranks 7th in population having 7.67% of total population. The state has 439 towns and 5.375 villages.

Tamil Nadu has a very long coast line of 1076 K.M. along the South east coast of India, cape in the South and a short distance on the South west coast of India. It has a continental shelf of about 41,412 sq.km and an estimated off-shore region of 22 lakh hectares, with the coastal stretch affording excellent scope for fishing operations throughout the year. The major rivers flowing in Tamil Nadu are the Cauvery in the Coramandel coast, the Vaigai in Palk Bay coast and the Thamaraparani in the Gulf of Mannar region. The fishery resources in these coastal waters have been traditionally exploited. The area up to 50 M depth constitute 23,255 KM and from 50-200 M depth constitute 18,157 KM. The entire fish catch is from within distance of 35 KM and upto a depth of 75 M.

ANDHRA PRADESH

This coast is stretching up to Antavedi covers a length of 126 KM. This stretch encompasses two district namely Krishna and

West Godavari. This stretch forms a bay and creeks, and is intercepted by several river mouths of Krishna and Godavari and a few other drains. Kolleru lake is an important fresh water lake covering the water spread area of 900 Sq.km, situated about 35 KM from sea coast. The Kolleru lake drains into the coastal water through Upputeru canal. The estimated brackish water suitable for fish farming is in the 9 coastal districts of the State. Penaeid prawns are cultured in the areas of Godavari estuarine complex, the estuaries of Srikakulam district and in and around Kakinada. The development of organisations such as the Bay of Bengal Project (BOBP) and Marine Products Export Development Authority (MPEDA) has actively involved in propagating brackish water fish and prawn culture in the state at Machalipatnam and at Neilerravu about 75 South of Kakinada. The saline ground water found in the Gurujanapalli pengudu belt located about 8 to 10 KM from Kakinada has been found to be suitable for aquaculture of prawns. There are about 27 coastal villages with a total population of 74.320 and out of this 16,413 are engaged in Marine fishing. The total annual fish catch is 4.11.360 tonnes which include both marine as well as fresh water fish. There are potential eco-systems for brackish water aquaculture in the state, offering wide scope for aqua-farming. If properly utilised these resources which are available will offer immense scope for aquaculture development.

FARMING IN BRACKISH WATER

The natural brackish water bodies connected with the sea can be classified as follows:

(a) Filtration Farms-are the shallow brackish water impoundments which are being auto-stocked with natural seed through high tide and are being harvested by filtration method.

(b) Extensive culture farms (EC) are the shallow impoundments which are stocked with natural and artificial seeds and the stock are usually harvested when they attain marketable size.

(c) Intensive culture farms (IC) are the shallow impoundments which are utilized for culture on scientific lines. In this case, extra care is taken in selection of location, seed, stocking, density, preparation of farms, feeding etc.

The inland brackish water areas which are used as productive prawn/fish farms are provided by necessary infrastructures such as finance, construction technology, seed, dependable farming systems, fertilizers and feeds. Trained manpower are available for culture which involves trapping naturally occurring wild young stock of varying periods for growth and harvesting. Salinity is the important single factor that determines the suitability of the area for farming. Suitable conditions prevail from September to April making possible to harvest two crops in a year. Third crop is possible in only those estuaries which have connection with the sea and even in such places may also find it difficult to mobile funds required for aquaculture development of the magnitude possible. This phenomenon, in fact, is the basis to sustain the recruitment of larva of commercially valuable fauna. Although the prawn and fish spawn in the sea, the habit of the larva and juveniles is to migrate into the estuaries and back waters along with the rising tide. The larva distribute themselves in the brackish water area depending on the required salinity range i.e. from 5% to 25% and grow into adult, but return to sea before attaining sexual maturity. Similarly, some of the fresh water larva forms too grow in brackish water medium and return to their parental niche to attain maturity. Therefore, the brackish water medium is suited more as a nursery for larva and juveniles but acts as permanent resident area for limited number of species only.

Since, the larva and juveniles migrate enormously into eco-system the occurrence of larval biomass that is available at our disposal as natural seed resources, is to be properly utilised towards aqua farming in India. As per the available figures, total area under shrimp farming has increased from 65,100 ha in 1900to1,86,710ha in 2003 (MPEDA-2003) and production from 35,000 t to 63,300 t during same period. The average annual growth rate of area is 8.9% and that of production is 26.1%.

FARMING IN FRESH WATER

Fresh water is a simple medium which can be handled easily as it does not involve maintenance of salinity to rear fauna. Further farmers located at different inland areas, i.e. river banks, valleys and hills have an easy access to make use of this medium. It is strange to note that, despite regular demand for fish as food in inland areas there is not enough effort put in to culture fresh water fish in the cultivable areas. Only selected establishments like Fisheries departments alone go for fish farming that too for a few notable species.

SCOPE OF AQUACULTURE

Aquaculture is a thriving industry in India since the traditional bulk of shrimps caught in the seas have resulted in over-fishing beyond the capacity and the seasonal availability along with rising operational costs have brought about the stagnation of sea-caught shrimp. At the same time the increasing demand for white meat in the International market and the availability of shrimp culture technology has resulted in the upsurge and rapid growth of aquaculture, thus making the horizon of aquafarming shin full of promise.

India successfully carried out two major revolution namely the 'Green Revolution' and the 'White revolution' and these revolution have saved the country from a major disaster of food and milk shortage. The only major natural resource that is left out, is the fishery resources of country and it is the 'Blue Revolution' when the new industry like coastal aquaculture emerged and brought a revolutionary change in the rural economy.

Aquaculture is now undergoing rapid development in order to:

1. Utilise the extensive areas which are now unutilized but which have possibility for aquaculture activities.
2. To increase the production of animal protein to meet the needs of the fast growing population.

3. To develop special market oriented products for export and increase foreign exchange.
4. To create employment opportunities in a labour surplus economy.

Traditionally, the culture of shrimps has been practised in estuaries, extensive back waters, tidal inlets, creeks and mangroves swamps, lagoons and coastal regions especially in Kerala, Karnataka, West Bengal and Goa without causing any environmental problems. With the increase in demand for prawns and shrimps in the foreign market, many corporate bodies and enterprising entrepreneurs have entered into aquaculture activities in order to reap quick profits.

SYSTEMS OF CULTURE

Culture systems of prawns and shrimps are broadly classified into the following based on the level of scientific management and nature of inputs.

Traditional

This system of culture is practiced in Bherries of West Bengal and Pokkali fields of Kerala from time immemorial. In this system shrimp seed along with fish seed are trapped during high tide in large impoundments and are allowed to grow. Artificial feeding is not done. Periodic harvesting of both fish and prawn is done during full moon and new moon periods, using traps/ bag nets. The production under this system is unpredictable. It generally ranges between 200-300 kg per ha per crop.

Improved Traditional

This system is like the traditional system, but has stock entry control. There is supplementary stocking with desired species of shrimp seed, (mainly *P. monodon or P. indicus*). This system is practised in small ponds of 2-5 ha.

Extensive

New ponds of 1-2 ha. are used under this method. They are tidal fed, with no water exchange, and are stocked with seed. Local feeds such as clams, snails and pond side prepared feed using soya, oilcake, cereal flour or wet dough in ball form are used. Here the stocking density is around 20,000 per ha.

Modified Extensive

In this system pond preparation is done with tilling, liming and fertilisation. Water exchange, to a certain extent, is done with the help of pumpsets. Imported or indigenous pellet form feeds are used. Stocking density in this type of farms is around 50,000 per ha.

Semi-Intensive

New ponds in the size of 0.25 to 1.0 ha. are used. Pond preparation methods are carefully adopted. There is elevated ground with supply and drainage canals. Regular and periodic water exchange is followed. Pond aeration with the help of paddle wheels at 8/ha. are used for air circulation. Generally imported feeds with Food Conversion Ratio (FCR) of 1:1.5 or more is used. As otherwise high energy indigenous feeds are used to feed the young shrimps. Drugs and chemicals are applied as and when needed. Stocking density is around 15-25 numbers per square meter of hatchery reared postlarvae (PL 20). The average production under this system ranges from 2 to 4 tonnes per ha per crop.

Intensive

Ponds are sized between 0.25-0.5 ha. Other pond management techniques are like the semi-intensive techniques. Four aerators are used per pond. Salinity manipulation is also resorted to. There is a central drainage system to remove accumulated sludge. Imported drugs are used. Drugs and chemicals are applied when there is need. Strict control and management is exercised. Stocking density is 30 to 35 numbers per square meter. The production level under this system ranges between 8 to 15 tonnes per ha per crop (Alagarsami, 1995).

Super Intensive

Super intensive culture system involves concrete ponds of 0.01 to 0.02 ha with continuous flow of very good quality water adjusted to suitable salinity. The stocking density is further increased to 30 to 50 nos per Sq.mt. and fed with pellatized feed. The production levels ranges from 10-20 tones per ha, per crop. The semintensive, intensive and super intensive are not per mited after supreme court judgement

DEVELOPMENT OF SHRIMP FARMING IN INDIA

Though shrimp farming by traditional method has been practised in India since long, the commercial-scale shrimp farming using semi-intensive method started only in late 1980s and early 1990s with the setting up of several large ventures in coastal regions of Andhra Pradesh and Tamil Nadu. India, though a minor player in total sea food trade, enjoys a fairly prominent position in the world shrimp market. It accounts for 12 per cent of the total world production of shrimps and commands an 8 percent share in world trade in shrimps in terms of exports.

The technical improvements made in shrimp farming in many parts of the world through research and development have paved the way to increase shrimp production in India through aquaculture by adopting intensive and semi-intensive systems of shrimp farming in areas which are suitable for taking up shrimp aquaculture. Shrimp farming has been given 'extreme focus' status in our national plans in the late eighties and early nineties to increase exportable production. India is endowed with rich natural resources in the form of brackish water and estuaries for taking up shrimp culture in the coastal zone of our country. The estimated potential brackish water area available in our country is about 1.2 million ha., of which we are utilizing around1,54,600, mostly adopting traditional practices (50,000 ha.) and partly by scientific extensive methods. (Aquaculture Authority website 2003).

The traditional systems of shrimp farming is carried out in the states of West Bengal, Kerala, Karnataka, Goa in an area of 50,000 ha. One crop of paddy cultivation during rainy season (low saline period) and one crop of shrimp during December-January to May-June are carried out regularly in the same field. Under this system, after the harvest of paddy, the incoming tides along with the young ones of shrimps and fishes that co-exist in the environment are trapped in the same field adjacent to brackish water estuaries and harvested at frequent intervals. Since the field are autostocked there is no control over the quantity and quality of seed stocked in the ponds. The stocked animals are also not allowed to grow to marketable size and the productivity under this system is often very low, ranging from 200 to 500 kg/ha/season (6 months). However, there is an interest in some areas for improving the productivity of these traditional farms by way of adding supplementary inputs of seed and feed. The recently developed new areas, under private sector in Andhra Pradesh, Orissa, Tamilnadu, Kerala etc. have attained production level ranging from 500 to 2000 kg/ha/crop through extensive methods of shrimp farming. Small and marginal farmers have achieved production level of 500 kgs/ ha /crop. The progressive farmers have achieved production up to 3,000 kgs/ha/crop in 4 to 5 months culture period. Some business houses have achieved a production of 4,000 to 5,000 kgs/ha in a period of 120 to 145 days culture.

MPEDA has also demonstrated the success of semi-intensive technology through field demonstration up to 4-5 tonnes/ ha/ crop at Nellore through the financial assistance given by the Department of Biotechnology. The highest production of more than 10,000 kgs/ha/crop has been achieved by some of the progressive entrepreneurs in Tuticorin area of Tamilnadu by adopting intensive methods. The annual production of cultured shrimps has been estimated to be around 1,45, 770 mt. In 2003, the production of cultured shrimp and scampi was 115320 MT and 30450 MT. In 2005-06 it has increased to 143170 MT and 42,820 MT respectively.

More and more new areas are being added every year as more entrepreneurs are entering into this field. A number of integrated aquaculture units with 100 per cent export oriented status have been set up in the country. Most of the state governments have also liberalised the leasing policies and are taking necessary steps to lease out the brackish water lands available in the coastal areas for shrimp farming development.

2

PROSPECTS OF AQUACULTURE OVER THE PAST

The status of aquaculture in India in the past decade was remarkable and many experts have analysed the augmentation of aquaculture in various ways. Some of their analysis are furnished below:

Raman K. and Gopinathan K. (1986) have analysed the "Prospects of Prawn Culture in Tamilnadu" in which five species suited for culture viz. *Penaeus monodon* (tiger prawn), *P. indicus* (White prawn) *P. semisulcatus* (Pasiyera), *Metapenaeus monoceros* (Poochi yera) *and M. affinis* were taken for their culture possibilities and techniques. They have pointed out that prawns are the principal exchange earner among our marine products which have an ever increasing demand in foreign markets. The study revealed that prawns are very sensitive to pollution. While giving artificial feedings, care should be taken not to leave excess feed in the ponds as it will lead to bottom pollution and mortality of prawns. Prawns being bottom feeders will be immediately affected. The nursery grounds must be kept free from human interference like industrial, agricultural and thermal pollution and also in discriminate reclamation. Govt. agencies may be required to attract public attention towards this lucrative industry.

P. Vedayasa Rao (1986) in his study "The Present status of the prawn fishery of India"-A Review , indicates a review of the investigations carried out on the biology of the commercially important prawns of India and the present status of the exploited prawn fishery of the country. It stated that India ranked top in the export trade in 1979 earned foreign exchange of 2,62 crore rupees in 2002-03, it is Rs. 6881.31 crores where in 2002-2003, it is 6881.31crore rupees. The annual marine production of the country during the past ten years period has been of 1,67,663 tones, forming 11.9% of the total marine fish production. Penaid prawn contribute to about 62% of the total prawn landings. The development and expansion of prawn fisheries of India over 30 years have been rapid by the discovery of production fishing grounds in the inshore belt of the coast, introduction of mechanised fishing boats, and modern techniques of bottom trawling, establishment of processing units have contributed to progressive development but this process of development has brought in several problems concerning conservation and management of the exploited prawn stocks for the continued sustenance of the fishery. The study stated that prawns are fished from the estuaries as well as from the sea and since their life is interdependent in these environments it is natural to accept that their capture from one environment affects the fishery of the other, so protective measures have to be framed to protect these areas from the developing agro industrial complex and the associated pollution for the better development of the prawn fisheries.

Jancy Gupta and K. Asokakumaran Unnithan (1990) have analysed in their study "Scientific prawn culture in homesteads-A gainful self employment opportunity for coastal women" that the role of women in aquaculture is relatively a new one which offers great scope for self employment and serves as an additional income to the family. The concept of prawn culture in home stead water canals is developed. Women constitute an important human resources of India's coastal areas. Their activities are mainly shore based activities such as post harvest operations like prawn peeling, fish curing, drying and collection of prawn seeds from back waters and surf zone. They are engaged as wage corners of earning a very low income. The authors have pointed out some of the guidelines for women who take to prawn farming in their home steads on these while selecting culture sites, care should be taken that they are connected directly or indirectly with backwater, having free tidal water movements.

Krishnan M, Vasisht A, K. and Sharma B.M. (1991) in their study, indicated that Maharastra contributes the maximum shrimp landing in India followed by Kerala. The study showed that the percentage distribution of total shrimp landings among the different states of India in 1986, were Maharastra 54.03%, Kerala 14.36%, Gujarat 11.31% Tamilnadu 6.29%, Andhra Pradesh 5.31% Karnataka 2.65%. West Bengal 2.16%. Goa 1.97%, Orissa 1.47%, Pondichery 0.34% and under mines 0.11%. The total shrimp landings in India had increased from 1,73,737 tonnes in 1980 to 1,96,716 tonnes in 1986. In their study "Growth Geographical Distribution and import peretation of Shrimp exports from India" have analyzed the export of shrimp from India. The study shows that the composition of shrimp exports has increased during 1976-86 but the growth of export earnings from the shrimp could not be maintained during 1980-86 due to lack of modernisation', lack of coordination between production and export, and lack of infrasturctural facilities. But in 2002-2003 the export of shrimp was 1,34,815 MT source (MPEDA).

According to Pillay, T.V.R. (1992) the rapid increase in aquaculture production in the world has raised fears of degradation of the aquatic environment, both in the industrially advanced as well as developing countries. Because of this, many governments and financing agencies now insist on environment impact assessments for permitting new aquaculture development programmes. He analysed the available information of the environmental aspects of various aquaculture systems, ranging from scenic beauty and socio-economic to ecological changes and genetic dilution of aquatic communities. It provided a valuable preparation of environmental impact assessments of aquaculture projects, and has shown that how environmental problems can be reduced to mitigated by sound management.

R. Sathiadhas, K.K.P. Panikkar and A. Kanakkan (1992) have analysed in their study "Costs and earnings of Trawl operations along Nagapattinam coast of Tamilnadu" that marine fisheries sector of India has undergone a rapid change during the last three decades. The introduction of synthetic nets coupled with export demand for shrimps has intensified fishing along our coastal waters. The lucrative external market for shrimp and constant rise in the mechanised trawl fishing fleets not only enhanced the marine fish production of our country but also showed the way for the growth of an organised sea food export industry and increase in employment opportunities in the subsidiary sector.

Panikkar K.K.P. (1993) has studied the Socio-economic analysis of prawn farming in Orissa state. The base line of the study was conducted on a comprehensive socio-economic survey of the beneficiaries of the cultured ponds.The size of family, the literacy level of the population, the occupational pattern, social problems, the economic of prawn farming, cost and earning data have been obtained. The average quantity of prawn produced in a pond of 0.2 ha in different districts were taken, the marketing problems mainly because of the defective marketing system and lack of infrastructure facilities the price realised are very low. By improving the marketing efficiency, the average revenue per crop could be raised. The farm income received from one crop from a pond of 0.2 (ha) in different districts has been highlighted in his study.

R. Kothandaraman (1994) has stated in his paper "Aquaculture Growing demand for Shrimps" that there is growing demand for shrimps in sea food and point out India's edge and certain relevant factors to ensure India's sustained growth. According to him for growing shrimps the most important input is a proper location. It should be facilitate unlimited and unpolluted saline water and correct temperature. India enjoys certain inbuilt advantages to be a leading player in this industry worldwide. He concludes by stating that this industry is basically an biological one and it is not likely to cause any major pollution as the let out water can be treated for avoiding any environmental pollution. But there should be discipline amongst the aquaculturists, since they can pollute themselves and therefore spoil the industry. To prevent diseases, proper water management, farm management, and health management of shrimp and feeding programme are necessary. This increased realisation will increase the profitability and sustained growth of the industry in India.

Krishna Srinath, A.M. Mohana, K.P. Salini, Manual, K. Sanhotra and A. Kanakkan (1994) have analysed on the extension of prawn culture technology to women in a coastal village. The study shows that prawn farming is a potential area of income generation for women in fishing villages. Observations indicate that women in small- scale prawn farming households do have involvement in the traditional system. They also play an important role in the management of other activities such as livestock rearing and vegetable cultivation in their farms, give more information and training they can be usefully involved in the adaptor of the technology and also management of the farms.

Manual Sridhar (1994) in his paper emphasizes the importance of the development of prawn feed industries and the dissementation methods adopted and the technological advances made in achieving the goals of low cost practical feed formulation from locally available low cost ingredients and also working out the economic viability of supplemental feeding.

Akio Kanazawa (1995) has explained in his paper "The recent developments in Shrimp Nutrition and Feed Industry on grow-out feeds" that feed is an important component in rearing of shrimps. Efficient food and diet is required for growing prawns which will accelerate the growth of the animal and also make the environment disease free. He recommended nutrient composition such as protein, essential fatty acids, phosphilipids, Vitamin C, attractants, Micro Nutrients, etc. essential for the growth of shrimp. Micro particulate diets are used for similar prawns due to their smaller size.

Alagarswamy K. (1995) in his study "The Indian experiences of impact of environment on shrimp farming, impact of shrimp farming on environment and the impact of shrimp farming on shrimp farming" (Auto-Pollution), stated that the case study in the Kandaleru Creek in Andhra Pradesh carried out by Central Institute of Brackishwater Aquaculture (CIBA) has revealed impacts due to the high nutrient load, increased Biological Oxygen demand (BOD) and Chemical oxygen Demand (COD). In order to avoid the recurrence of the environmental problems, ecological management of shrimp farming was emphasised. He suggested the recommendations of "National workshop on sustainable development of shrimp farming" to be adopted by all.

Bal A.S. (1995) in "Environmental issues of shrimp farming "stated in the study carried out by them for MPEDA on environmental management of shrimp farming the external and internal Environmental factors which effect the shrimp farming activities and points out the control measures for the shrimp farm effluents and explained a conceptualised treatment system to control the effluents affecting the environment. He also emphasised the need for establishing three `C's namely Co-operative shrimp farming, Common effluent treatment system and Conservation of nature.

Dehadrai P.V. (1995) has emphasised in his study 'Stabilisation of Aquaculture Industry in India' that India has a vast potential for exportable fishery resources, from marine sector in which the export of fish and fish products has crossed the U.S. 1 Billion mark during 1994-95. Total quantity of fish and fish products exported during 1994-95 was 0.3 million tonnes. However, the exports in fishery sector are limited to certain preferred marine fish species. The quantity of export though steadily rising at enviable rates of growth, the country would have to make several efforts towards increased production particularly when the marine fish production trends are indicating a picture world over including India. The gap between the demand of the rapidly increasing global population and the stagnating production of capture fisheries, that has to be bridged over by aquaculture production. He pointed out that marine capture increased its production more rapidly than the population growth. Alternatively, the inland fisheries particularly aquaculture has tremendous potential for achieving the sizeable quantum in fish production. The aquaculture has been attracting heavy investment with sound technologies available and limitless potential for export especially for shrimp. Under aquaculture much more land and water could be included. In addition about 0.9 million of coastal land awaits utilisation through brackish water farming for shrimp. He stated that the growth of aquaculture in India has been rather smooth when compared to that in other countries and emphasised that the aquaculture needs to be diversified.

John Kurien (1995) analysed in his study "Fisheries and people unsuring the coastal commons" that the unregulated entry of foreign capital into our marine fishery will sound the death-knell of the livelihood of local fishing communities.

He stated that marine fisheries in India is as much about people as it is about fish the coastline provides a livelihood to the population density in the coastal zones of our maritime states. The author states that some drawbacks due to the change in the structure of access to the sea, by the sudden transformation of a subsistence sector of economy into a potential money spinner in the face of the lucrative profit expectation coupled with the infusion of a modern technology. The unregulated entry of new source of capital into marine fishery areas has lead to a decline in the harvest of other fish species by unregulated trawling for prawn.

R. Parthasarathy (1995) has stated in his study "Aquaculture continuing Controversy" that aquaculture to some it spells prosperity, while others see in it a veritable threat to the environment. An undisguised craze for striking "Aqua Gold" has lead violent protests from environmentalists and social activities because of the environmental and socio-economic problems arised out of the unplanned and indiscriminate setting up of shrimp farms. He also points out that while the sweeping "blue revolution" has ushered in economic prosperity to shrimp farm promoters in general and a few corporate giants in particular, it has wrought an ecological disaster, with the desertification of fertile lands in villages abutting the shrimp farms which poses danger to the very livelihood of farm labour and fishermen in the coastal belt of Thanjavur and Nagapattinam-Quaid-E-Millet (NQM) districts of T.N. State.

In each of the seven villages, shrimp farms setup along the coast in the past two years had wrecked havoc on the ground water quality leading to serious environmental degradation. A majority of the shrimp farms openly flouted environmental guidelines by discharging untreated effluents into neighboring lands and endangering the fertility of their lands. Not only the farm workers suffer a loss of income, fishermen too find their traditional access to the sea cut off as the shrimp farms have laid huge inlet pumps to bring in sea water to fill the shrimp ponds, many drinking water sources in adjacent villages have turned saline due to indiscriminate pumping of groundwater by shrimp farms.

The harmful effects of the effluents discharged by the hatcheries and ponds depend on the quality and quantity of the discharge, culture stage and the type of farming adopted. The impact is not much if the hatchery is being operated on a small-scale, but discharge from large-scale, extensive, semi intensive and intensive hatcheries are likely to cause problems. He concludes by saying that Dr. M. Sakthivel, President of the Aquaculture Foundation of India (AFI), asserts that aquaculture is not polluting industry. He also refuted the charge that the discharge of untreated effluents into the sea affected marine life. He claimed the aquaculture presented a golden opportunity to usher in a "revolutionary change" in the life of coastal villages. He also suggested to the Government to regulate the shrimp farms.

Santhanakrishnan G. (1995) has stated in his paper "The Shrimp aquaculture scenario in India" that with a potential of more than 1.2 million hectares of land is at our disposal,only 7% is being utilised for shrimp farming, that too more than 50,000 ha in traditional farming confining to the Ganges delta for *P. monodon* production and adjacent area of Vembanand backwaters for production of white shrimps and about 30,000 ha is under scientific farming. He also pointed out that under the present context in Kandaleru creek in Andhra Pradesh there is a need for studying the carrying capacity for optimum stocking. He highlighted the Report of National Environmental Engineering Research Institute (NEERI) carried out on environmental management for prawn farming activities. Finally he emphasised the need for setting up effluent treatment system for treating the effluents.

Swaminathan M.S. (1995) in "Environmental issues of Shrimp farming" has stated the need for sustainability of shrimp farming. He emphasized on adoption of environmental friendly aquaculture taking into account social, environmental and economical angles. He finally emphasized the following aspects for its sustainability e.g. location, construction, production and post-production management aspects. The areas of concern should be prioritized in order to harmonize the sector with the environment. He also stressed the need of ecological farming.

The fishermen density in this inshore zone will naturally depend on its physical area of, which each maritime state depends on the length of the coastline and the distance of the 50 metre is a bath from it. (MSY) Maximum sustainable yield of fishery resources from our Exclusive Economic Zone (EEZ) have been placed at about 3.9 million tonnes, of which around 2.3 million tonnes are found in the inshore zone and the rest in the area beyond (called the offshore-upto the 200 metre in so bath and beyond that depth called the deep sea). The over all density of the fishery resources in the inshore zone is around 11 tonnes per sq.km and in the sea beyond 6.5 tonnes per sq.km. The bulk of the commercially valuable fishery resources is concentrated in the inshore sea.

Marine fishing, has from time immemorial, been the privilege of certain coastal communities over the centuries and the fishing communities have always viewed the seas as "Mother" and "Provider". The sea is hence the integral and life-giving source to the community. This unwritten, privileged, access rights of the community to the sea and the living resources there in were trampled over by the modern state which developed a variety of technologies tailored to the specific ecological riches along the coast. Prior to Independence, the British did take some interest in the fishery as part of their over all effort to increase wartime food supplies. They made attempts to introduce improved fish processing techniques and set up the first formal administrative and revenue collection structures in the govt with the required legislative measures to introduce change in the industry. The World's first development project was the Indo-Norwegian Fisheries community development project (INP) located in the state of Trivancore in 1951.

He also states that some drawbacks due to the change in the structure of access to the sea, by the sudden transformation of a subsistence sector of economy into a potential money spinner in the face of the lucrative profit expectation coupled with the infusion of a modern technology. The unregulated entry of new source of capital into marine fishery areas has lead to a decline in the harvest of other fish species by unregulated trawling for prawn. The inshore environmental damages and the concentration of purse seining in large harbours has resulted in a major dislocation in the decentralised, unsegmented, local level employment structure in the fishing villages and also a decline in the wide spread availability of fish for local consumption in the coastal areas of the two states. After 1982 a widespread socio ecological upheaval in the coastal villages and the establishment of a militant, independent artisanal fishermen's trade union which was able to pressure the state to introduce fishery management and social welfare measures for protecting the rights and improving the livelihood condition of the artisanal fishermen. It also highlights the role of coastal fishing communities must play as "beacons of the sea" in monitoring these conditions. They are environmental impacts affecting fishery marine resources and fishing communities, which originate outside. The marine eco-system, being "tail end" ecosystem, the coastal inshore zone is affected by pollution and degradation associated with all human activities in the "up-stream" eco-system. The post-1991 economic policies of the Govt. of India and the invitation to foreign concerns to enter agri-business in the form of "joint ventures" has lead to a more "Open seas" policy in marine fishing. He concludes by saying that the entry of foreign capital will result in conflict with the small-scale fishermen a corollary of the adverse ecological impact and conflict over resources will imply conditions unimical to the livelihood of coastal fishermen and a severe shortage of fish for local condition.

In recent years, fishery science and technology have made tremendous advance. The increasing role of aquaculture in the production of large variety of fish as a source of food have completely revolutionsed the knowledge of this science and helped to meet the increasing global need of food. Aquaculture is a dependable source for the supply of good quality fish and represents one of the cheapest and effective sources of high quality animal protein. It also provides large scale of employment to fisherman without the conventional hazards of professional fishing.

These articles provides comprehensive and authentic knowledge of vast discipline of fisheries and aquaculture.

The Hindu (Jan 25 1998) records an official as saying that the central and State Governments are not to allow the prawn farm owners to revive the farms which posed grave threat to the environment, besides rendering several thousands of agriculture workers jobless in the Nagapatinam district. He added thousands of acres of cultivable land in the state had been spoiled due to the setting up of the farms in the coastal districts. A large number of agricultural workers, a majority of whom were dalits, had been deprived of their livelihood as agricultural operations were affected in these areas.

Though Supreme Court has ordered the closure of the prawn farms, the pro-form lobby has been actively working to make the governments revive them through a law, he said and added that the Govts. should obey the Apex Court order instead of succumbing to such pressures.

The environmentalists were not opposed to setting up of eco-friendly fresh water prawn farms.

The Hindu (Oct. 15, 1998) shows how the Integrated freshwater aquaculture in woodlands is an ecologically sound venture and an economically viable proposition. It offered good scope for efficient recycling of organic farm residues. The fish pond serves as a water harvesting and storage structure and helps in saving crops during prolonged dry spells, according to export.

The farm-ponds in gardenlands and the paddy-cum-fish culture in wetland are ideal for raising composite column feeders and bottom feeders. Improved varieties of fish such as catla, rohu, mrigal grass carp, silver carp, cat fish and freshwater shrimp are the most commonly grown fish.

In the integrated farming system, crop and livestock enterprises are also blended perfectly to enhance farm productivity and profitability.

Introducing ducks in the ponds can help in aerating the ponds, installation of light traps for monitoring crop pest, will be highly beneficial to aquaculture. The trapped months that fall into the water will be readily devoured by the fish. Dried and wet blood meal from the poultry and slaughter house can be fed in small quantities for fresh water shrimp.

The Hindu (Jan.29, 1998) records, "The public opinion should be around against the Aquaculture Authority Bill, now pending before the Lok Sabha". The farms, which had been set up for earning a few dollars, had resulted in widespread degradation of the environment, alienation of thousand of acres of fertile land, unemployment of farm labourers, salinity of water, high levels of toxic pollution of water bodies and coastal water and destruction of coastal ecosystems and fishing villages. After five or six years these farms would become barren, unfit for any purpose.

The Hindu (March. 25,1999) shows how the need for an environment impact assessment of all projects activities along the coast is required if our bio-diversity is to be preserved, it was emphasized at a meeting was held on 'environmental law and coastal land pollution. The exploitation of natural resources without taking into account, the environmental impact on habitat could spell doom in the future.

On aquaculture farming along the coast it was initially operated under the head of agriculture but with time the dimensions of the activity became more industrial. Recalling a Supreme Court judgement which took into consideration the 'cost benefit analysis' of this enterprise, it was found to have lost its agricultural character. The coastal water was getting polluted due to the chemicals used to better yield.

The New Indian Express (June 3, 1999) record the interim report of the Home Committee set up to study the impact of prawn cultivation on environment in the coastal belt of the state should be immediately implemented.

The committee which was headed by then Revenue Minister K.C. Lenka had recommended that all intensive and Semi intensive prawn culture should be legally banned in the state pending formulation and adoption of a long-term aquaculture policy, keeping in view the provisions contained in the environment act 1986 and the Supreme court orders.

The members of the legislative assembly pointed out that the House Committee had strongly supported the demand for prohibition of Prawn culture through strict enforcement of the provision of Orissa Land Reforms Act and stopping auction of sairats (Fishery sources).

The Hindu (June 14, 1999) records the information on Supreme Court had issued order banning activities in prawn farms two years ago. But many prawn forms continued their activity violating the court order.

One lakh areas were not with prawn farm owners. Most of the land thus acquired by the farms remain barren without any activity. Such land should be taken back by the Govt. and distributed to landless agriculture labourers. Sea erosion at many places of tourist importance such as Poompuhar, Mahabalipuram, Tiruchendur, was causing concern. It could be prevented by raising mangrove forests which also act as habitats for fish, prawn, etc. Presence of prawn farms in such sensitive coastal places threaten the environment he has said.

The Hindu (June 27, 1999) reports informed that the Orissa Govt. has decided to ban prawn culture in the Chilka Lake. The decision comes in the wake of the recent agitation by the traditional fishermen demanding demolition of all types of 'gheries' made in the lake for prawn culture. The Govt. was considering a fresh fishing policy for Chilka lake in the light of the Supreme Court order on the issue.

About the on-going demolition of gheries in Chilka the Govt hoped to remove all gherise at the earliest of the 20,281 acres encroached by the 'Prawn mafia" in Puri district, gheris in 10,223 acres had been demolished by May 31, in the year 1999.

In Khurda district, 1,250 acres of the lake had been covered by gheries. The 432 acres had been cleared. All the gheris in Ganjam district had been demolished.

The Hindu (June 28, 1999) report shows that how the Orissa High Court has stayed State Govt.'s decision to demolish and dismantle the prawn "gheris" in the Chilka lake till June 30. Four persons had died in police firing at Sorana in connection with the demolition of prawn gheris in the lake. Subsequently, the State Govt. issued a notification on June 18, for demolition of all gheries in and around Chilka lake.

The New Indian Express (July 1, 1999) reports shows how the Tamil Nadu Grama Swaraj Movement chairman has appealed to the Prime Minister and Chief Ministers of all coastal states to implement the Supreme Court judgement and save the coastal boundaries from environmental pollution and exploitation of millions of people.

The Sarvodaya leader stated "The two coastal boundaries of the country, the eastern and western coasts, are invaded by multi national prawn companies trading and finally enslaving the country. The poor working people, millions of fisherman and farmers living in the areas are at the merciless exploitation of the multinationals and the lives of these people are at peril"

The movement appealed to the State Govt. to take over the thousands of acres occupied by Prawn companies part of the land fit for cultivation which was lying waste and also the lands used and salivated by Prawn culture should be reclaimed by scientific process and distributed to the landless.

The Indian Express (July 1,1999) reports informed that the leaders of all political parties in Orissa have agreed for a "Prawn Gheri-free Chilka lake" favouring a ban on prawn culture in the largest brackish water lagoon in Asia.

A complete ban on prawn culture be enforced in the lake in the wake of the Apex Court and the Orissa High Court

Judgements. The court has also demanded that the lake be made free from encroachers.

The New Indian express, July 12, 1999, reports stated that the Aquaculture Authority "Public Notice that Aquaculture Authority has been set up as per the directives of the Hon'ble Supreme Court which is functioning under the administrative control of the Ministry of Agriculture. The Authority has been set up to deal with the situation created by shrimp culture activities in the coastal areas and to regulate shrimp farming activities. The Authority has already set up district/State level committees for processing applications received from the shrimp farmers seeking approval of the Aquaculture Authority.

A public notice was issued in this regard in all the leading newspapers during 20th to 25th Feb., 1998 requesting shrimp farmers operating traditional and improved traditional systems of shrimp culture, willing to adopt improved technology for increasing production to apply in the prescribed format for the approval of the Aquaculture Authority. Shrimp farmers already operating outside the Coastal Regulation Zone(CRZ) and those who want to set up new farms outside CRZ were also asked to apply in the prescribed format and obtain authorisation from the Authority within a specified period. Undertaking shrimp culture activities in coastal areas (other than traditional and improved traditional) without the proper approval of the Aquaculture Authority. Set up for this purpose, shall be in violation of the Supreme Court's Directives.

It is hereby informed that those who have not so far applied for approval of the Aquaculture Authority for undertaking the above mentioned activities should apply to the concerned authorities immediately and in no case later than 31st July 1999. Failure to file application within the prescribed time would be dealt with severely as per the provisions of the Environment (Protection) Act, 1986.

The Hindu Nov. 1, 1999 Reports that the Union Ministry for "Environment and Forest (MOEF) Will be reviewing the Coastal Regulation Zone (CRZ) notification nine years after it came into being because it feels the notification has not fulfilled the aspirations of the people of coastal areas. It plans to `elaborate and clarify several clauses of the notification" in order to remove the deficiencies in the existing policy, for the purpose, the Govt. Has sought World Bank assistance and help from other related and private sectors in the country.

The Indian Express Nov. 1999 reports that aquaculture developments are a cause for enviornmental concern. Rapid expansion of shrimp farming destroys mangrove and marsh areas. The wastes generated by these farms increase the organic load in the tidal canal and adjacent areas of the sea resulting in environmental deterioration".

Environmental protection authorities could priortise their work on four different leads on (a) quality (b) impacts (c) politics and (d) economics. Legislation could also be accompanied by economic disincentives that penalise polluting industries. Aquaculture and environmental revolutions have a common feature where by sustainable global economy is essential.

The Hindu (Nov. 9, 1999) report shows how the National Bank for Agriculture and Rural Development has expressed concern over the delay in starting the process of issue of licences to coastal aquaculture units in Tamil Nadu under the coastal zone regulations. One of the officials of the financial Institutions said that several other states had issued licences promptly to units after constituting the coastal zone regulatory authority in terms of court orders.

The loans given by the banking system in the case of such units would become irredeemably lost unless the operations were allowed to be resumed early. In some cases, prawn farms had been demolished under the orders of revenue authorities. Mr. N. Raghavan Executive Director of NABARD said corporate brackish water prawn units were unlikely to be allowed in future but mainly small ponds especially in the coastal regions, would be allowed the state should also break the stagnation in freshwater aquaculture by setting up demonstration units.

Aquaculture is gaining momentum in India. Severe Shortage of freshwater has limited inland aquaculture. Waste water aquaculture is a branch of aquaculture, where the processed waste water or the treated effluent is used for fish production. This paves way for not only earning a sizable income from the effluent, but also helps in reducing the objectionable matter present in the effluents.

Both organic and inorganic effluents can be biologically treated. Compared to inorganic effluents organic effluents can be effectively treated and biologically and specific group of bacteria and algae can effectively utilise organic and inorganic matter as their food. This will help in reducing the load to a considerable level. Installation of a bio-filter pre loaded with beneficial bacteria is essential for biological treatment of waste water. Passing the effluent water through these bio-filters at determined flow rate would ensure complete bio-degradation. Apart from microbes, aquatic plants and certain alage can also be used in effluent treatment. Select group of aquatic plants have the capacity to utilise the minerals and metals present in the water. Aquatic plants through their absorption of objectionable elements make water biologically suitable for fish culture survival of aquatic organisms in the treated water itself is an index of the quality of the effluent water. Effluent water, if free from harmful chemicals, can be used for aquaculture purpose. Hardy fishes can be selected for cultivation. However, application of biological treatment has to be done after careful analysis of the effluent.

3

ECONOMICS OF OVER EXPLOITATION OF NATURAL RESOURCES

NATURAL RESOURCES

Environmental and natural resource issues are closely linked. Nature provides the resources that humans use. Mining copper from the ground can have environmental impacts. Extracting that copper today means that it cannot be extracted in the future, and its price may change given the interactions in the economy, that may lead to greater use of substitutes for copper and different sorts of environmental impacts. Whereas some resources, like copper and oil, are finite and exhaustible, others can renew themselves. If trees cut today are replanted, there will be trees to cut tomorrow- at least up to a point. Often the same market breakdowns or lack of well-defined markets that leads to environmental impacts lead to inefficient use of these renewable resources and sometimes to their irreversible depletion.

SUSTAINABILITY AND SUSTAINABLE DEVELOPMENT

How sustainability and sustainable development are incorporated into workable environmental policies is not always clear. As Toman and others point out, there are different and conflicting definitions of sustainability. Forming workable policies to achieve sustainable development goals cannot be designed if there is no agreed definition. In other words, there is no single unit of account, like money, that can measure whether or not a country's development is sustainable. Advocates of sustainability often argue that we should limit our use of all natural resources and that economic development should be based on the use of renewable rather than exhaustible resources. Yet how much the current generation should limit its own use of resources is not clear. One of the most difficult issues with sustainable development is the necessity to confront the need to allocate scarce resources. Choosing between saving whales and saving salmon from extinction, for example, still requires that scarce resources be allocated (Lesser & Zerbe 1995).

INTERNALIZING EXTERNALITIES

Internalizing an externality through private transactions will take place when three conditions are met. First, there must be technically feasible gains from trade. Each party must be able to provide something the others want at a lower cost than the others could provide it on their own. This condition will always be met when we encounter an externality. For example, in theory, store owners could sell clean air that could be purchased. One of the attributes of an externality is that it causes potentially feasible gains from trade not to be realized.

Second, a transaction must be institutionally feasible. There must be a way for the parties to agree on a formal or informal contract within the existing legal and institutional structure. It must be possible for them to define the terms of an agreement. To define the rights and obligations of each party, to set forth their natural expectations, and to specify recourse if obligations are not met. In short, there must be well defined property rights in what ever is to be traded, and there must not be institutional and legal structures that prohibit the particular type of trade. Slave trading, for example may be technically feasible, but in most countries it is not institutionally feasible.

Third, the affected parties must be able to capture at least some of the gains from trade or atleast not be harmed by the trade. The exchange must be a pareto superior one, as no party will enter voluntarily into an agreement that harms that party.

In sum, the costs of negotiating and enforcing an agreement, the transactions costs, must be less than the gains from trade for each of the parties. The key public policy question that the existence of an externality raises is whether or not there are institutional changes that will improve the situation. This may at first seem starting because it leads us to consider "optimal' amounts of pollution. That concept troubles many individuals (e.g., Kelman 1981) because, many individuals have goals other than improving economic efficiency.

When all potential gains from trade have been realized, there is no externality. The conditions for this to be realized are started formally by what has come to be known as the Coase Theorem (Coase 1960: Zerbe 1980).

If there are well-defined property rights for all goods and services and zero transactions costs, the equilibrium allocation of goods and services will be efficient and there will be no externalities. The lesson Coase himself seemed most anxious to impart is that the mere existence of economic interdependence does not mean that there is an externality, nor even if there is an externality does this imply that corrective action is needed. Coase started that an action would be efficient only if it lowered transactions costs, the affected parties could reach a mutually beneficial resolution and turn interdependence into an opportunity rather than a problem.

EXTERNALITIES AND PROPERTY RIGHTS

Ownership of property can be thought to involve the right to exclude others from its use, the ability to sell the property, and the rights to use the property. The degree of ownership can be defined by the strength of these qualities. Allen (1991) defines transactions costs as resources used to establish and maintain property rights. Externalities often involve incomplete property rights or ownership. No one owned the right to clean air or water in the sense that they could charge or restrict polluters.

In some cases, the absence of property rights may be a matter of public policy. For example, Ault and Rutman (1989) note that private property in land arose only as land became scarce, where as previously the costs of defining private property in land had exceeded the benefits. In other cases, many societies have placed restrictions on the buying and selling of land, requiring that ancestral land be kept in a family or limiting the amount that one person could own. Historically, in the United States, incomplete property rights were developed for water resources. But as water has become more scarce, it has become more worthwhile to develop a private property rights system. Property rights may be ill defined because they are unenforceable or untradable. In many cases, there are social or legal restrictions on certain trades. In the United States for example many western states have tied ownership of water to ownership of land and placed restrictions on the sale of water for use off the associated land. In other cases, property may not be tradable because of inconsistencies between formal property rights and physical reality. This is often the case where property rights are defined in a way that ignores the impacts on third parties.

Some Western States have experienced with defining water rights in terms of consumptive use, the amount of water that is diverted from a stream less the amount that returns downstream. For irrigation, this is the sum of water that is used by plants, that is lost to evaporation, and that percolates into deep aquifers. Defining ownership of water this way makes it a tradable commodity, but water sales based on consumptive use rights can have major impacts on third parties downstream. This is because return flows from irrigation typically travel through shallow aquifers and reemerge downstream over a period of several months, and selling upstream rights to consumptive use can change the timing of water availability downstream.

Before two or more people can negotiate any new arrangement of rights and obligations, they need an initial set of rights and obligations and they need a framework of behavioural norms and expectations, including sanctions for violating the norms. If those do not exist (i.e., if there are no property rights), they must be invented as part of the negotiations. Thus when property rights are undefined, the costs of negotiation will be high.

EXTERNALITIES AND A FIRM'S SUPPLY FUNCTIONS

The supply curve of a profit-maximizing firm is the upward sloping portion of its marginal cost curve. When a firm's production process creates external costs or benefits, the firm will base its supply decision on thc costs that it pays, not on the social opportunity cost of its output. The marginal cost paid by the firm is called its marginal private cost to distinguish it from marginal social cost.

When a firm's production process has external costs but no external benefits, marginal productive cost will be greater than marginal social cost. One reason for this is obvious. The firm is not paying some of the costs of its production. Marginal cost is defined as the change in input cost with a change in output:

$$MC = \Delta\, TC/\Delta\, Y = \sum_{i=1}^{n} Pi\, \Delta\, Xi/\, \Delta\, Y \tag{1}$$

Where X_1,——X_n are the inputs used in producing the output Y. If X_n is an unpriced input such as atmospheric waste disposal, it will be left out of marginal private cost;

$$MPC = \Delta\, TRC/\Delta\, U = \sum_{i=1}^{n} Pi\, \Delta\, Xi/\, \Delta\, Y \tag{2}$$

We have just seen that externalities in production will distort a firm's input choices. Thus the input quantities X_i in the equation 2 are not the socially optimal quantities X_i^*. Marginal social cost, as defined by the production possibilities frontier, is

$$MSC^* = \Delta\, TSC/\Delta\, U = \sum_{i=1}^{n} \pi i\, \Delta\, Xi^*/\, \Delta\, Y \tag{3}$$

Where each π_i is the marginal social costs of the ith input. However, with the firm making non-optimal input choices, the cost actually paid by society is

$$MSC' = \sum_{i=1}^{n} \pi i\, \Delta\, \overline{X}i/\, \Delta\, Y \tag{4}$$

Where the $\overline{X}$ are the firm's actual inputs. Usually MSC'>MSC*, but this is not always the case/ it is always true that total cost of any given output is greater with non-optimal inputs, but the cost of some increments of output may be lower. Suppose that contaminated water discharged from an industrial plant damages a fishery. MSC* reflects the damage to the fishery that would occur with an optimal water treatment system. This damage may not be zero, but it will be lower than the damage with untreated effluent. MSC' reflects the damage to the fishery with untreated effluent. Now suppose that at some pollution level, the fishery is wiped out. Increases in production and pollution beyond this point will have no additional costs on the fishery. However, with optimal water treatment, there would still be a fishery to damage and MSC* would be greater than MSC'.

The result of these differences between.MPC and MSC is that a firm whose production process has external costs will supply more than the optimal amount of its output at every price.

LIMITS TO GROWTH

The major cause of environmental damage has been our quantitative growth, or economic scale, and our resulting consumption of ecosystem space. Global deforestation is most alarming. Leaking and Lewin reviewed two independent studies by the World Resources Institute and the United Nations Food and Agriculture Organization, each reporting deforestation rates in the range of 80,000 square miles per year. At this rate, tropical forests may be reduced to 10 per cent of their original cover early in the 21st century.

Contemporary arguments for an absolute limit to this unprecedented human growth began with the report of The Club of Rome's Project on the Predicament of Mankind. The Meadow's group constructed a computer model of exponential growth in population, industrial capital, food production, non-renewable resource consumption, and pollution, within geologically and geographically defined physical and social limits. Assuming the then-current rates of exponential growth, they found "the limits to growth on this planet will be reached some time with in the next one hundred years", and that the "most probable result will be a rather sudden and uncontrollable decline in both population and industrial capacity"

The Meadow's work highlighted physical, environmental, and social limits to growing material consumption as the causes of projected societal collapse. Unfortunately, the physical limits hypothesis (i.e., limits in energy and mineral resources, fresh water and arable land) became the most popular forecast of their larger body of work. Under their exponential index scenario, the world's reserves of copper, lead, mercury, natural gas, petroleum, tin and zinc were all predicted to be depleted within the seven year period 1985-1992. However, through changes in demand, increased recycling, substitution possibilities, and discovered geological reserves, limits to 20th century growth imposed by absolute scarcity were largely avoided. For this reason, the "limits to growth" hypothesis has more often than not been rejected by mainstream economists.

On the social front, demand for education, health services, and political stability continues to be greater than our ability to provide it to much of the global citizenry. The 1993 HDR 2004 is also one and Human Development Report is available on the net. Found for all developing countries (about 77 per cent of the world's population) a 40 per cent secondary school enrolment ratio, and 72 per cent, 68 per cent and 55 per cent of the population with access to health services, safe water, and sanitation respectively.

PROPERTY RIGHTS AND EFFICIENCY

Ownership rights to resources and product are important determinants of economic efficiency. The effects of a communal or common property right system for resource allocation have received the principal attention of contributors to the literature pertaining to fishery economics. Common property means that any member of the country has the right to harvest the fish stock. However, this right in practice may be constrained by government enforced conservation policies such as bag limits and size limitations. Consensus among the discussants is that common property leads to over-exploitation of fish stocks and perhaps extinction of the species. The property rights literature draws similar conclusions.

Open access exploitation of common property fish resources frequently causes severe stock depletion. Indeed, the question whether open access may cause stock extinction has been analysed by several authors (Smith,1968 and 1975; Berck 1979; Hartwick,1982). Moreover, as Smith (1968) has pointed out, although stock equilibrium under open access may be positive, the stock may be driven to extinction along the path of adjustment. Stock equilibrium may also be stable and positive with fixed prices and technology and still drift towards extinction over time, since these fixed variables drift in the long run.

With the exception of Wilen (1976) the work on the dynamics of open access or free entry fisheries is mainly theoretical. The purpose of providing an empirical application is based on the North Sea herring fishery. Open access exploitation of a number of schooling species has caused severe stock accumulation.

COMMON PROPERTY AND ECONOMIC EFFICIENCY

In a world, where transaction costs are significant and resources are scarce, common property right systems result in less efficient resource allocation than private right systems. This occurs because communal rights do not ensure that the costs of an individual harvester's actions in exploiting the resource are borne fully by him. In attempting to maximize the value of his common right, the individual can be expected to over exploit the resource leading to depletion of the stock, and in the extreme case to extinction of even replenishable resources. Private property internalizes the costs of the harvester's actions. In a similar way, a private right enables the producer to capture a greater proportion of the benefit of his activity in comparison to a communal right.

The type of externality manifested by communal rights to oysters depends on the stage at which the production process is being examined. In general, an oysterman can separate production into two stages: establishment of suitable conditions for oysters to mature, and second, the act of harvesting oysters for market.

Other things equal, an individual could transform barren subaqueous land into productive grounds by depositing rock or shells on to it. He could then plant seeds on the material to hasten maturity. It should be obvious, however, that this kind of activity is minimal unless the planter is given the exclusive right of harvesting oysters from that land parcel. Under a communal right system, such a guarantee is non-existent.

Three problems arise at the harvesting stage. First, the harvesting process typically removes cultch. Unless replaced, cultch removal implies disinvestments. On communal property once again, incentive to replenish this material is minimal. In practice, most states stipulate that some proportion of shells be redeposited on communal oyster grounds. In many states, however, processors rather than harvesters bear this cost. Frequently, states also subsidize the communal system by undertaking cultch rehabilitation programmes. Second, overcrowding of vessels on particularly rich water areas leads to congestion. Finally, immature oysters are caught indiscriminately with the mature. Consequently the growth behaviour of the stock is affected. Most states set a minimum size restriction and require that culling of undersized oysters be done immediately upon being caught. Culling restriction are also accompanied by stipulations that any cultch that was removed by the act of harvesting also be replaced immediately.

Given the variety of external costs associated with communal rights, it remains an empirical consideration as to whether the enforcement of private rights is economically feasible. It has been noted that in the case of migratory fish the policing problem may make exclusive use rights unmanageable. In the case of non-migratory species, however, property rights seem practical. In the case of sessile species such as oysters, private property rights are lively to incur minimal enforcement costs. Indeed, private rights have been instituted and enforced in all states to some degree.

COMMON PROPERTY RESOURCES AND AQUACULTURE

Many resources can regenerate themselves, if given the chance. Depletion of such renewable resources is a major environmental policy issue; spending to restore endangered Columbia River Salmon has run into hundreds of millions of dollars each year, and concern over destruction of the rain forest has encompassed everything from the loss of potentially valuable species to destruction of native people's habitat to changes in the earth's climate.

Almost all major fisheries are open-access, or at least common property resources. There is a far more uncertainty associated with stock levels, for keeping track of what moves about under the ocean is far more difficult than surveying what remains standing on land. Nevertheless, there are numerous policies that can be used to manage such common property resources efficiently.

EXTINCTION OF A FISHERY BY COMMERCIAL EXPLOITATION: A NOTE

Development of the literature by Smith (1969) has greatly increased the power and generality of the economic theory of commercial fishing. In contrasting his own analysis with previous work, Smith suggests that the most serious deficiency in the received doctrine is that "it is not able to handle the situation in which a species may be exploited to the point of extinction. The theory implies that short of zero unit costs the equilibrium yield to competitive exploitation is never zero with an extinct population".

As Smith observes, evaluation of this implication depends on whether one believes that commercial fishing has ever, or could ever, cause the extinction of a fishery- a matter over which there is some controversy.

The "Traditional" Theory of Fishing: Standard theory is formulated in terms of long-run, or steady-state, equilibrium, and the following is a summary account.

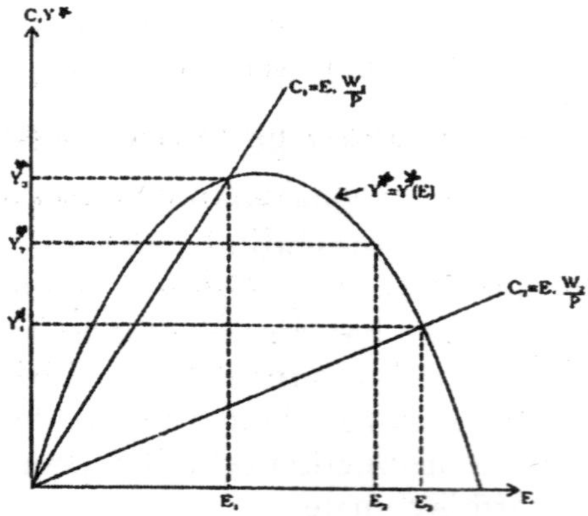

Figure 1

Following the direction set by Gordon's seminal paper (1954), models of fishing examine the interaction between the fishing industry and the fish population. The economic equilibrium of the fishing industry depends on the size of the fish population, and the biological equilibrium of the fish population depends on the size of the fishing industry. Full, or bionomic, equilibrium requires simultaneous equilibrium of both the fishing industry and the fish population.

Biological theories suggest that, given certain parameters- such as water temperature, food supply, and the level of activity of natural and human predators- the fish population will grow to a definite equilibrium size. At this population level, there will be a determinate steady-state yield of fish to the given level of fishing effort. This is the "sustainable yield", in the sense that, in the long run, this rate of yield to the fishing industry will be exactly offset by the natural increase in the population, and both population and yield will remain stable if none of the parameters change.

If the level of fishing effort is very low, the population will grow to a large equilibrium size, but the sustainable yield will be small. At an intermediate level of fishing effort, the sustainable yield will be larger, even though the equilibrium population is smaller. At some high level of fishing effort, the population will have been so depleted that, once again, the sustainable yield will be low. Thus, it is argued, the sustainable yield is at first an increasing, then a decreasing function of fishing effort as depicted in above figure, where Y* stands for sustainable yield and E for fishing effort.

For simplicity of exposition, we shall assume that fishing effort is in perfectly elastic supply at cost W, and that the demand for fish is perfectly elastic at price P, assumption which are consistent with a small fishery drawing on a large pool of fishermen and serving a large market.

A characteristics feature of fisheries is that they are "common property" resources: no fishermen possesses rights of ownership which enable him to exclude others from exploiting the fishery. In these circumstances, fishermen will enter the fishery as long as the average product of effort exceeds their transfer earnings. In equilibrium, the average product of effort equals the real wage, and the rent attributable to the fishery is zero–that is, total revenue equals total cost.

Bionomic equilibrium, or simultaneous equilibrium of both the fish population and fishing effort, is illustrated in above figure. The yield of fish in response to effort is Y* (E), and the total cost curve is expressed in terms of fish by the equation $C = EW/P$. The zero-profit equilibrium condition, $PY = WE$, is represented by the intersection of C and Y*(E). when the supply price of effort is W_1, the total cost curve is C_1, and the equilibrium effort E_1. At a lower supply price for effort W_2, the total cost curve is C_2, and the equilibrium level of effort E_3.

The diagram indicates that, as the cost of effort falls below that consistent with C_1, the equilibrium yield will fall. But as long as the cost of effort is positive, the equilibrium sustainable yield remains positive- which implies a population greater than zero. This is the reasoning behind Smith's inference that the received theory rules out commercial extinction of a fish population, except at zero supply price of effort.

CONTRACTING PROBLEMS AND REGULATION: THE CASE OF THE FISHERY

The inefficiencies of common property fisheries are of continuing concern to economists. The early work by Scott

Gordon (1954) and Anthony Scott (1955) outlined the problem and later studies by James Cruthfield and Giulio Pontecorvo (1969) and Frederick Bell (1972) provided empirical estimates of the losses that result. Those studies were followed by the dynamic models of Colin Clark (1976), and James Quirk and Vernon Smith (1970) of optimal harvest rates and the use of corrective taxes or quotas to achieve them. But in spite of a large and growing literature and the persuasiveness of the outlined efficiency criteria, most fisheries retain common property aspects with over-capitalization and excessive labour input.

THE SHARE SYSTEM IN OPEN-ACCESS AND OPTIMALLY REGULATED FISHERIES

Although the share system is almost universal in fisheries throughout the world, it has received little treatment in the literature, the exceptions being papers by Zoeteweij (1956), Satinen (1979), and Griffin, Lacewell, and Nichols (1976). The latter shows that a share system can divide the rent from the fishery between vessel owners and crew members. The share system into the traditional static deterministic model of an exploited fishery is described in Gordon (1954), Christy and Scott (1965), and Anderson (1977). It is generally agreed that a main purpose of the share system is to spread risks between boat owners and crews.

Some Considerations of Population Dynamics and Economics in Relation to the Management of the Commercial Marine Fisheries:

Fishing is one of man's oldest occupation; some of the sea fisheries pre-date recorded history. So long as men relied on oar and sail to reach the fishing grounds, and on simple, hand-operated gear to catch the fish, the intensity of fishing on the high seas remained low, so that the amount of the catch had apparently little effect on the magnitude of the fish stocks. There were great variations in the harvests, of course, but these were due to fluctuations in the fish populations quite independent of the amount of fishing. A fisherman's success depended on uncontrollable natural factors, and was not much affected by whether the number of fishermen was many or few.

With the industrialization of sea fishing in the latter part of the last century, bringing steam and later diesel power to the vessels, and bringing new and more efficient types of fishing gear, and machinery to handle it, the sea fisheries in northern Europe and in some other parts of the world began to show signs of diminishing return per unit of fishing effort. Near the turn of the century, there was considerable controversy as to whether or not the amount of a given kind of fish which man is able to take from the sea is sufficient to have any noticeable effect on the supply. This matter was discussed at some length, for example by McIntosh (1899), Garstang (1900) and others. Alfred Marshall was preparing the first edition of his famous Principles of Economics (1890) at the time when the industrialization of the British trawl fishery was proceeding rapidly and this controversy was going on. It was, therefore, yet a moot question whether his law of Diminishing returns applied to the sea fisheries (Marshall, 8th edition, 1938, p. 166).

BIOLOGICAL ECONOMICS

Attempts to systematize some of the significant biological and economic facts bearing on the problem of how the amount of fishing should be managed in order to provide the greatest benefits to mankind have been made by a number of persons in recent years., among which may be cited Russel (1931), Graham (1935, 1939,1953), Beverton (1953), Gordon (1953, 1954), Burkenroad (1951), and Schaefer (1954a,b). The main result has been a considerable advance in our understanding of the biological and economic principles involved. There is, however, a fairly large degree of confusion, resulting from the biologists' inadequate consideration of economic principles, and, in part, from economists' failure to fully consider the properties of a self-renewing natural resource, the rate of renewal of which is dependent on the magnitude of the stock of the resources, which importantly distinguish such a resource from other classes of natural resources.

It seems worthwhile, therefore, to consider together some significant aspects both of the population dynamics of commercial fish stocks and of the economics of commercial fishing in order to arrive at a rational basis of considering the social problem of fisheries management.

In considering the bionomic properties of a fishery the main concern is with the "long run" relationships. That is, the main interest is in the average annual harvests that will be sustained by the fish population indefinitely at different levels of fishing effort, the monetary value of the harvests, and the monetary cost of the fishing effort. This approach has been admirably and carefully applied by Gordon (1954), but some further consideration appears to be necessary, because (1) he has not made the necessary distinction between the self-regulating, density dependent fish resources and other common property resources of a different nature, (2) the mathematical model in Section IV of his paper is not consistent with the assumption in Section III (and is not quite in accord with some dynamic properties of fish population), and (3) he has (p. 129) defined the optimum degree of utilization of any particular fish stocks as that which maximizes the net economic yield, the difference between total cost, on the one hand, and total receipts (or total value production), on the other. This is one possible choice, of course, but it is not immediately obvious that it is social optimum; indeed other possibilities have been explicitly chosen both for particular fisheries and as a general objective of fishery management.

THE RELATIONSHIP OF FIRMS PRODUCTION IN COMMON PROPERTY FISHERIES

Most of the previous work in this area (Gordon 1954; Scott 1955; Crutchfield and Zellner 1961; Copes 1970; Gould 1972a; Anderson 1973, 1975a, 1975b; and Clark 1973) has been in aggregate terms only. In the model developed by Smith (1968,1969) and in the interchanges between him and Fullenbaum, Carlson, and Bell that these works generated (Smith 1971,1972; and Fullenbaum, Carlson, and Bell 1971,1972), however the operation of the firm is directly taken into account. Because neither Smiths model nor the traditional literature deal adequately with changes in the level of firm output in the context of obtaining an industry equilibrium, Fullenbaum, Carlson, and Bell conclude, "The integration of the classical theory of the firm and the traditional theory of commercial fishing remains an unfinished task"(1972, p.768)

In a model that focuses attention on the level of fishing effort as the output of the individual vessels rather than on the catch rate as do Smith and Fullenbaum, Carlson, and Bell. This change in the frame of reference will make the analysis of vessels in a fishery strictly analogous to the standard firm-industry model and more important, more logical and empirically more useful. It is more logical because, while vessels can directly control fishing effort, they can only indirectly control vessel catch rate. This change then allows for a more explicit model. It is empirically more useful because it allows for the use of biological and physical information in a form already provided by fishery scientists and fishery management organizations. These strong statements notwithstanding, the generalized model that results from the analysis, to follow, although significantly different, is a modification of the basic model as presented by Smith. The benefits from completing this integration are a description of vessel operation while in the process of reaching a long-run industry equilibrium and a more complete analysis of regulatory problems.

The average and marginal revenue curves for effort for the fishery as a whole, $\overline{E}$ which equals KE, K being the number of vessels, are depicted in part B of Figure 2(b). They can be derived directly from the total revenue curves in Figure 2(a). Fishery–wide average revenue can be thought of as the derived demand curve for effort. Notice that as the total amount of effort in the fishery increases, the long-run average return to effort (i.e., the market's willingness to pay for it) decreases. This results not from a change in the price of fish (although if price were variable this would aggravate the problem as long as increase in effort leads to increases in yield)but rather to the bio-technological phenomenon of decreasing long-run

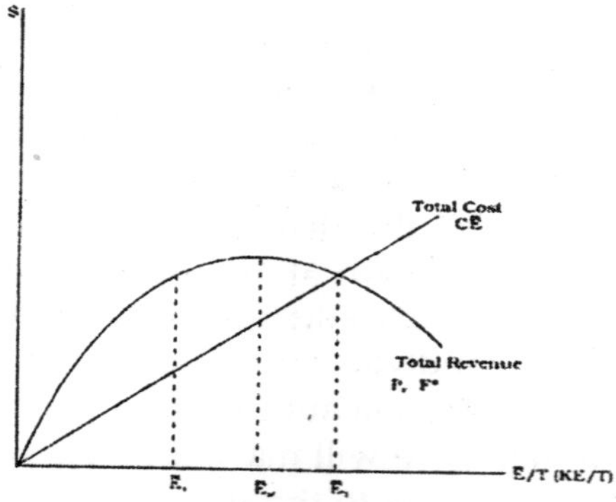

Figure 2a

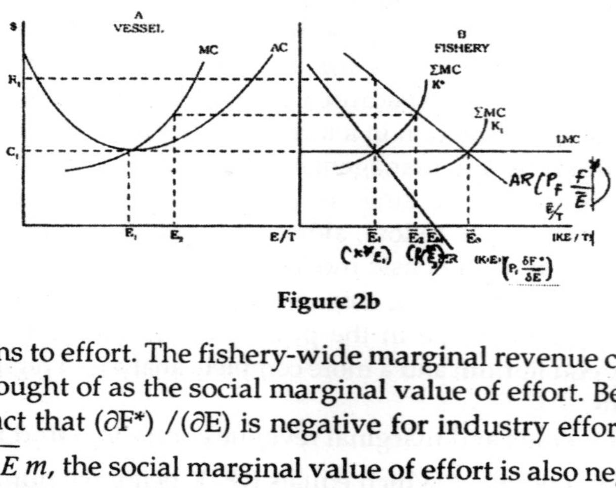

Figure 2b

returns to effort. The fishery-wide marginal revenue curve can be thought of as the social marginal value of effort. Because of the fact that $(\partial F^*)/(\partial E)$ is negative for industry effort greater than $\overline{E}\,m$, the social marginal value of effort is also negative in this range even though the derived demand is positive.

In the normal fashion the horizontal sum of the supply curves of the firms is the supply curve of effort for the fishery. For example $\Sigma/_{K_1MC}$ is the fishery-wide supply curve for effort when there are K_1 firms.

THE ANALYSIS

Using this format it is now possible to study the interaction of the fishery as a whole and the individual vessel. Very briefly the intersection of the fishery-wide supply curve for effort and the average revenue curve determines the average return per unit of effort (assuming a biological equilibrium is reached). This average revenue is the product of the average yield per unit of effort, which is an industry-wide phenomenon and the price of fish. Each vessel takes this as its perceived price or marginal revenue of effort (because this is what they will earn by selling the catch obtained by each unit of effort) and operates where the marginal cost of producing effort equals this amount. Of course, all of this occur simultaneously. Each vessel operates individually according to a perceived price which is set by all vessels operating in concert.

Open-access equilibrium of the fishery will occur at $\overline{E}_3$, with K_1 vessels each producing E_1 units of effort. At this point the average return to effort is just equal to the minimum average cost of producing effort by the representative vessel. If there were fewer vessels, the fishery-wide supply curve would shift to the left increasing the average return to effort. Each vessel would respond to this by increasing its level of effort until marginal cost equaled perceived price. The existence of greater than normal profits would, however, encourage entry of new vessels until average industry return is pushed down to the minimum average cost.

Maximum economic yield is where the value produced by the marginal unit of effort is just equal to the long-run marginal cost of producing it. Assuming no crowding externalities, the long-run marginal cost curve of the fishery will be constant and equal to the minimum of the average cost curve of representative firm i.e., additional effort can be assumed to be provided by additional boats each operating at the minimum of their average cost curves. MEY, therefore, occurs at 'E_1, where the long-run industry marginal cost curve intersects the fishery-wide marginal revenue of effort curve. Utilizing the normal interpretation of short-run and long-run cost curves, this means that in order to achieve MEY the number of vessels must be reduced to K* and that each of them must operate at E. At this point each vessel will be earning a rent of $E_1(R_1$-C1) which is its share of rent of the fish stock . It is not a monopoly rent. To see this, notice that at MEY the marginal cost of effort, $(\partial \text{ cost})/(\partial E)$ is equal to the marginal return to effort, (P_F) $(\partial F^*)/(\partial' E)$. This can easily be transferred to $P_F = (d \text{ cost}) / (d F^*)$; i.e., the price of fish is equal to the marginal cost of increasing sustained yield.

As a final point, note that this model allows one to describe the long run cost curve of the fishery. Open-access equilibrium effort will be produced as efficiently as possible because ultimately, any expansion will take place in the form of new units producing in an optimal fashion. (The common property aspect of the problem will not affect the long run cost of producing effort, but it will ensure that an improper amount will be used). And while it generates the same long-term result as the traditional analysis, at the same time it provides an analysis of how the vessel operators will, in a short run, alter their production levels in response to differences in their perceived price of effort and marginal cost, thus making the cost of effort increase at non-equilibrium points. It is this extra insight that gives rise to the restriction on vessel output listed above as necessary to achieve MEY. Note from the figure that if the number of vessels is restricted to K* but no controls are placed on vessel output, an industry equilibrium will occur at $\bar{E}_2$ with each vessel producing E_2 units of effort. This is the point where the perceived marginal return to effort is equal to marginal cost of effort given the limited number of vessels. At this point each remaining vessel will be earning more profit than at E_1. This increase, however, comes at the expense of efficiency in the economy as a whole because at $E_2(K^* E_2)$ the long-run marginal cost of producing effort is greater than its social marginal value. This means, of course, that optimal regulation will require constraints on effort per boat as well as on the number of boats.

Since the traditional analysis ignores variation in this effort-level of individual vessels, this policy recommendation does not follow. (As first pointed out by Turvey(1964) a general analysis of a fishery also requires regulation of mesh size).

An interesting example of this problem is the limited entry program in the British Columbia salmon fishery. The number of vessels was frozen with plans for a government buy-back program to reduce effort. (For a complete description of the program, see Morehouse (1972) and Pearse (1972). Initially, new boats could be constructed only if another was retired. In the first years of the program, however the average tonnage of the new vessels was three times that of the ones they replaced. Subsequently, the program managers have instituted a ton-for-ton replacement rule but are still finding that changes in the amount or composition of gear on each vessel is changing so as to increase the actual amount of fishing effort produced. In terms of this model a proper replacement rule should be in terms of the ability to produce standardized units of effort.

ECONOMIC AND ENVIRONMENTAL ANALYSIS OF MARINE FISHERIES

Growth measured in terms of GNP became a cult in the 1950's (Common, 1988, p. 17). This period coincides with the growth-oriented modernization programme in the fisheries of most developing countries of Asia, including India. In these countries the promotion of industrial fisheries and aquaculture was undertaken under export-oriented regimes and as part of the overall package of structural adjustment programmes (ICSF, 1996, p. 116). Economic growth continued to be in the forefront of economists' interest till the 1970's. But it has also been shown by economists that economic growth is not a cost free social objective(Galbriath, 1958; Boulding, 1966; Mishan, 1969; Daly, 1968 and 1973; Georgescue-Rogen 1971; Barkley and Seckler 1972; Victor, 1972; Lecomber, 1978). Deterioration of the quality of environment is one of the prices to be paid for. The most forceful expression of such a view came with the publication of the Club of Rome's mathematical model on "Limits to Growth" (Meadows *et al.* 1972). The depletion of resources is explained as synonymous with exactions from the environment and pollution has been identified as the insertions into the environment (Perrings, 1987, p-35). The environmental/ ecological economics literature has now sufficiently grown to analyse economy-environment interactions in a very comprehensive way.

Dasgupta and Maler (1991); Perrings (1992, 1994 and 1995); Constanza *et al.* (1993); Gadgil *et al.*(1993); Perrings and Pearce (1994); Perrings and Opschoor (1994); Berks *et al.* (1994); Holling *et al.* (1995); Folke (1995); Perings and Dalmazzone (1997); Bate (1968); Barkley and Seckler (1972); Savage *et al.* (1974); Dasman *et al.* (1974); suggest that "the ecological conscience" be incorporated into the process of economic growth in order to avoid an ecological catastrophe.

Fish is a bio-economic resource. Fisheries have the characteristics of the common pool resources in the sense that their consumption is rival but exclusion is difficult and costly to enforce (Smith, 1997, p. 53). When biological species become commercially valuable they are subjected to pressures from economic agents (Brown, R. 1998, pp. 3-11). The size of the resource stock (population) is determined jointly by biological factors and action taken by the society (Hanley *et al.* 1997, p. 3). The size of the population in turn determines the availability of resources for future. The flow of biological resources over time is not purely a natural phenomenon. In this context, fisheries management becomes crucial to regulate the resource over time and over generations (Bhattacharya, 2002. p. 62).

Because of the scarcity of, and competition for, the marine resources, attempts have been made to understand about the dependence of fisheries on marine environment. As per the evolution theory marine ecosystems are the most ancient life-supporting systems from which other natural ecosystems have evolved. Therefore, it is the most complex and unique ecosystem of the world (ICSF, 1996, p-5). It is believed that life on earth owes its past, present and future existence to the oceans. The bio-geographical interlinkages of the oceans unite us, while the land masses divide us (Kurien, 1998a, pp 30-32).

Oceanographers have pointed out the tremendous diversity of the bio-physical structures in the seas. They have divided the seas into three types of environment: (1) the coastal zone (2) the open waters over the continental shelf and (3) the deep ocean (Steele, 1998, pp. 33-36). Of these the coastal zone plays a crucial role in sustaining fisheries and aquaculture. The coastal zone includes lagoon, river mouths, coastal low lands and areas over which the influence of the sea is directly experienced ((ICSF, 1996, p. 7). Two-thirds of marine fish production come from stocks which pass the initial and most vulnerable stages of their life cycle in coastal areas. The coastal zone is characterized by a rich diversity of natural habitats, such as coastal and mangrove forests, coral reefs, reef flats, continental shelf areas, sand dunes, grass lands, marsh lands, rocky shores, salt marshes, estuaries, mud flats, wetlands and sea grass beds.

A variety of natural resources, including corals, seaweeds and algae, fish, minerals such as lime and salt, sand, oil and gas provide food, fuel, construction material and other resources indispensable for human existence. Coastal habitats and resources are also vital because of their role in stabilizing the shoreline, and in protecting coastal areas and habitations from cyclone, tidal waves and other natural disasters, as well as because of their natural capacity to assimilate and absorb 'waste' and 'pollutants'. There are also diversity of natural processes occurring in coastal areas, such as upwelling, seasonal sand banks, sand dune formation, sea erosion, siltation and sedimentation, the lunar and diurnal cycles, seasonal sounds and cyclones, sea breezes, waves, tidal bores and flows, salinity changes and seasonal migration of fish and birds, all of which contribute to maintaining the coastal ecosystem in complex and often unknown ways.

Fisheries are similar to other systems of economy-environment that are only partly controllable and partly observable (Perrings, 1991, p. 276). It is now generally accepted that an ecosystem become unstable if the biophysical stocks rise above or fall below some critical threshold. Stocks harvested may also be complementary with the remaining stocks in the system, which if ignored may lead to the collapse of the system (Perrings, 1991, p-281). Economists who support the control approach for natural resource management hold that prices are inadequate signals of the environmental processes (Dasgupta, P. 1982, p. 1; Perrings, 1991, p. 275). They argue for environmental stabilization based on direct observation of the physical systems and imposition of physical restrictions on economic activity. A precautionary approach is called for in using and managing such resources given the state of inadequate knowledge.

Figure below represents the marine economy-environment interactions.

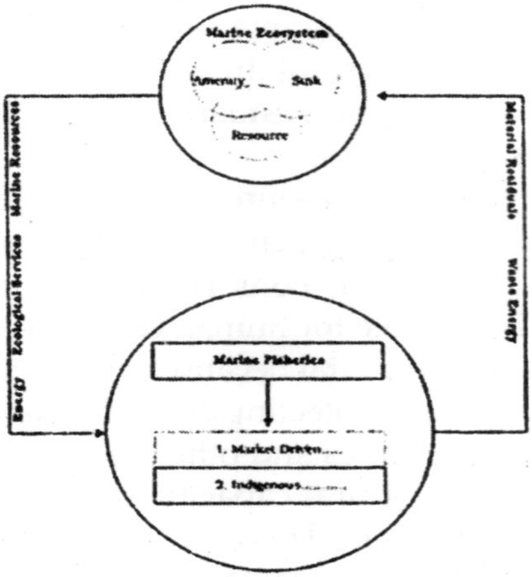

Figure 3

Three cycles representing the functions of marine environment overlap reflecting the fact that they interact and may be competitive (Common, 1998). The capacity of ecosystem to fulfill any of these roles is not unlimited (Freeman et al. 1936, p-10). The marine economy has dualism. There exists a traditional small scale unorganized sector with household as the production unit, along with the growth-oriented, market-driven, modern organized sector. The relationship of the traditional sector towards marine resources is one of dependency of sea for survival. The organized sector on the other hand considers sea as one of the many resources to be exploited to gain maximum profit in the shortest period possible. Indefinitely prolonged fisheries expansion may be impossible on account of the finite nature of the stock. Growth becomes progressively more difficult to achieve as the ability of the natural environment is impaired.

The growth curve in the Figure 4 reaches a maximum and declines thereafter with increasing efforts in fishing. The marine environment is impacted by the production and consumption activities of modern fisheries. The dynamics of the marine fisheries are not independent of the systems. Loss of ecological resilience implies reduced ecosystem stability (Perrings, 1994, p. 1). The use of destructive technologies causes disruption of ecological linkages and species extinctions (Field, 1997, p. 30). The cost of increased productivity in the organized sector is the loss of resilience in the marine ecosystem (Perrings, 1994, p-13). Because of the inter-linking of species and processes in the marine environment, harvesting of the species, especially some key-stones species, affects many other species, initiating the process of depletion of biodiversity. Perrings (1995) has observed that by depleting population, it is possible to disrupt a wide range of economically important ecological services.

The unorganized sector uses appropriate labour-intensive technology. It has established a permanent relationship with nature. Fishing is done as household enterprise undertaken in pursuit of a livelihood leading to a culturally conditioned way of life. They fish primarily in the coastal waters using small craft and simple gear of relatively low capital intensity. Their fishing operations are skill-intensive. Fisherfolk have an

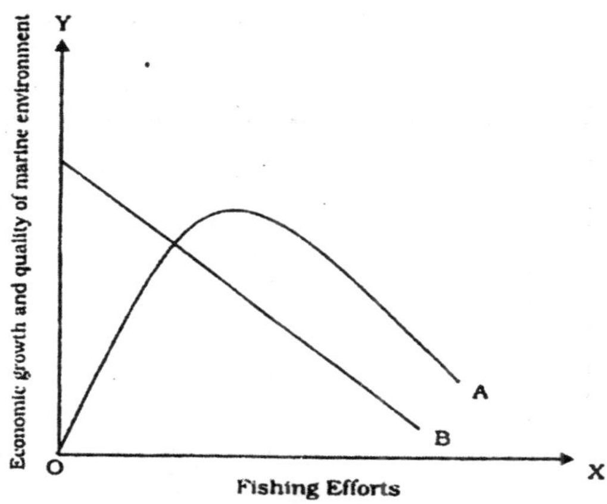

Figure 4

intuitive understanding of the coastal aquatic milieu and the fishery resources in it. The traditional ecological knowledge (tek) and skills are passed down from generation to generation. They are linked to locally oriented market networks. The internal driving force of the fisherfolk is towards sustainability. The sensitivity of fisher people towards the health of the marine environment helps them not to overexploit the resources therein as it would disrupt the harmony of the ecological system and their economy. They live within the limits imposed by the environment as they vie the sea and its resources as intergenerational social capital (Perrings, 1990, p. 144). The fisherfolk personify the sea as a mother, generous to the children who respect her and harsh to those who do not. There seems to be apparently no growth in their economies as per modern standards of growth. However, if the dynamism and resilience of the marine ecological systems are considered their economy, though apparently not growing, is very sound. Such a situation is depicted in the following figure, where economic growth and environmental quality (resilience) are represented by parallel lines.

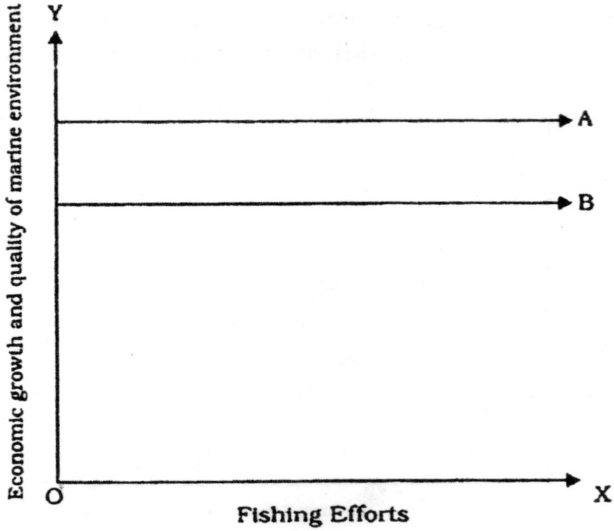

Figure 5

This shows that the marine fisheries economy and environment are well integrated and sustainable in the traditional sector.

Theoretical studies related to marine fisheries are mostly based on the relationships between species stock levels, growth functions, harvest rates, effort and fish catch. Some of the selected studies on fisheries include Gordan (1954), Schaefer(1957), Gulland (1978), Dasgupta & Heal (1979), Dasgupta (1982), Wilson (1982), Lawsen (1984), Pearce and Markandya (1990), Perrings (1991, 1992, 1995), Perman et al. (1996), Hanley *et al.* (1997), Kasulo and Perrings (2000).

Gordan(1954) deals with the determination of static equilibrium of an open access fishery. The theoretical models developed in response to the apprehensions arising from over exploitation of fish population are the probabilistic (stochastic) model and the analytic model. Clark (1976), Smith (1977), Dasgupta (1982) and Perrings (1991) have analysed the operational rate of harvest of fish species through the control approach model. The control approach identifies an operational resource management policy and established the necessary and sufficient conditions for such an operational policy. Wilson (1982) provides a critique of the traditional bio-economic theory of fishing economics. According to Wilson (p. 417) fisheries tend to be a highly valuable multi-species system with imperfectly understood biological and social dynamics. Perrings and Kausalo (2000) developed a model of equilibrium analysis for the multi-species Malawi Fisheries.

In fisheries economics management has emerged as a crucial subject. Number of studies are done at the national and international levels on the subject. The concept of maximum sustainable yield (MSY) is used as a target reference point in fishery management. It was first formulated in the Schaefer's logistic model in 1933. Larkin (1997) has studied on the evolution of the concept and Barber (1988) examined the reasons for the continued use of MSY in fisheries management.

ECOLOGICAL ECONOMICS OF MARINE FISHERIES

According to the United Nations Food and Agriculture Organization (FAO) world fish production including aquaculture, reached an all time record of 1270875 million tones does not include scampi or freshwater shrimp in 2002 (FAO, 2002). However, the global demand for fish continued to increase. Despite improved landings in some regions, supply has failed to much the demand. The ever-expanding consumption of the world's people in the highest income countries causes growing depletion and degradation of renewable resources that undermine the livelihood of the poor(World Bank,1998).

ECONOMICS OF FISHERIES

Fishery resources are capable of regenerating themselves so long as the environment in which they are nurtured remains favourable. Although the stock of fish resources can grow, it can also be exhausted if conditions interfere with the productive capability of the resource, or if rates of harvesting continually exceed natural growth (Perman et al. 1996, p. 169). A distinction can be made between stocks and flows of the fish resources. The stock of population is considered as the measure of the quantity of the resource existing at a point of time. The flow refers to the change in the stock over an interval of time. The change results either from biological factors, such as the entry of new fish through recruitment or exit from the population due to natural death or from economic factors such as harvesting of the species.

The combination of human-made capital, labour and fish stocks define a fishery production. Fishing effort measures the capital, energy and labour devoted to fishing during a particular time period. It might be measured by the number of boats operating in a fishery on a particular day. The economics of fishery resource exploitation concerns with the nature of the production function, where effort devoted to fishing, interact with a natural population to give a harvest rate. It is also concerned with the effect, which property rights have over a fishery. The open-access status of many marine fisheries leads to the over exploitation (Pearce and Markandya, 1990, p. 250).

Fish resources can normally survive as a species indefinitely so long as the stock is not depleted below a certain level. But excessive rates of catch, leading to the bio-mass falling below the species threshold level can result in the permanent destruction of the species (Dasgupta and Heal, 1979, p. 113; Dasgupta, 1982, p. 3).

In the absence of effective government regulation or some other form of collective control over harvesting behaviour, open-access resources tend to be over-exploited and there is a likelihood of the resource being harvested to the point of exhaustion.

The theory of fish resources exploitation has been built upon the basis of biological and economic models. These models are gradually being improved in order to make them more suitable for application. The basic logistic form of biological growth function was developed and first applied to fisheries by Schaefer (1957). The objective of biological models is to establish for the fish resources, the point of maximum sustainable yield (MSY). It refers to the point at which the fishing level will be at its biological optimum with no threat of resource depletion. MSY has been considered the most important technical reference point for the rational exploitation of fishery resources. Fishing mortality(F), Stock bio-mass(B), are the most often quoted basic reference variables.

The Schaefer growth model describes the linear relationship between effort and yield to provide a smooth symmetrical curve. According to this model, total yield increases as effort increases to the point of MSY. After that point an increase in effort leads to a fall in total yield because of over fishing. The biological growth function of fishery resources describes the growth process of one species at a particular location. The environmental milieu in which the stock exists, determines the population's growth possibilities. It is assumed that the ecological characteristics of the environmental milieu remain constant. Under these static assumptions the growth function can be expressed through a simple equation. If St denotes the mass of the resource stock at time t, the amount of growth of the resource, G, is a function of the resource stock itself

$$Gt = G\ (St)$$

The rate of growth of the stock can be written as dst/dt = G (St)

The biological growth function which can be approximated to the natural growth processes of many fish is the logistic growth function. It indicates the stock level which depends on the carrying capacity of the environmental system. The equation for the logistic growth function of one species at a particular location is

$$G(S) = gs- gs2\ /\ S_{MAX}$$
$$\text{Or } G(S) = gs\ (1-s)\ /\ S_{MAX}$$

The co-efficient g is a growth rate parameter, and S_{MAX} is the maximum stock size that can be supported in the environmental milieu. The equation shows that the amount of growth G, is a quadratic function of the resource stock size.

If the environmental milieu remain constant S_{MAX} is the maximum size to which the biomass can grow. S_{MSY} is the maximum stock size at which the quantity of net growth is maximum. Accordingly, resources could be managed in which yield of a certain size could be taken in perpetuity while maintaining the stock size at the fixed level S_{MSY}. Since this is the largest yield that could be obtained from the resource, it is denoted as the MSY. Thus steady-state equilibrium is possible in which both harvests and stocks are positive. Constant amounts over indefinite periods of time can be taken. Open access does not necessarily result in fish resource exhaustion. A steady state harvesting of fishery resource exits when all stocks and flows are constant over time. The harvest level is fixed over time and is equal to the natural amount of growth of the resource stock. Addition to and subtractions from the resource stock are thus equal, and the stock remains at a constant level over time. If the demand for the resource is constant over time, the resource net price will remain constant in a steady state, as the quantity harvested in each period is constant. However, it is also possible that open access conditions do lead to the stock levels being driven to zero. There may be some critical level of the stock, S_{MIN}, which is essential for survival of a particular population of a species in one environment. The species can gradually die out if the stock falls below S_{MIN} and reproduction is less than natural mortality (Perman et al. 1996, p-170).

The minimum sustainable population stock S_{MIN} in the figure 3.6(a) is shown as occuring at a zero stock size whereas in the figure 6 (b) the minimum sustainable population stock, S_{MIN}, is some positive quantity. The particular fish species would collapse to zero if the stock were to fall below the minimum sustainable stock, S_{MIN}.

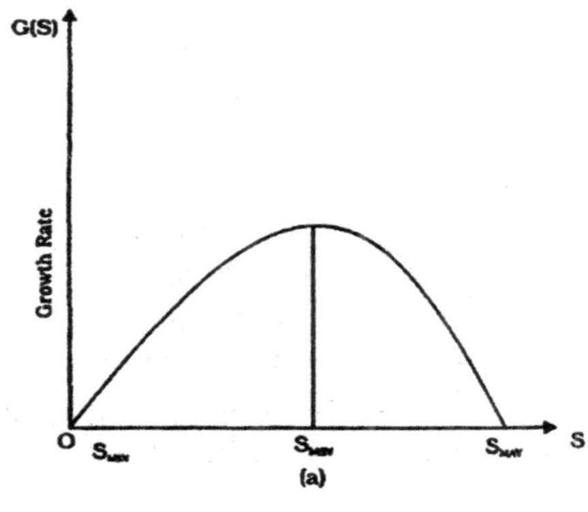

Figure 6a

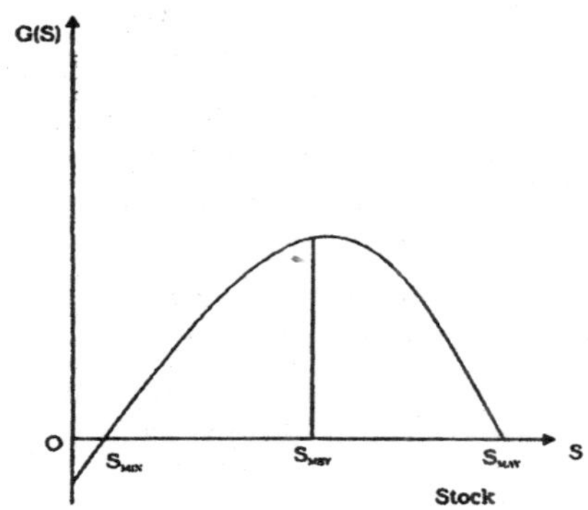

Figure 6b

Improvements on the Schaefer model have been made by the dynamic pool model (DPM). This model refines the static assumptions of Schaefer model, as to the growth and composition of fish stock and considers that there is a constant movement in the size, composition and level of recruitment to stock due to various causes. The knowledge of recruitment rate, growth rates in weight of fish, the probability of death from natural causes at different ages. From these data a more accurate estimate of MSY may be obtained for appropriate fisheries management and it may be possible to sustain a level of fishing without threatening depletion of stocks (Lawson, 1984).

Gordon, H. Scott (1954) presented an economic model of fishing in which fish catch is related to fishing effort, corresponding to a given stock of fish. Gordon also pointed out the possibility of over fishing in an open economy. In the literature on the economic theory of the fisheries the Gordon Schaefer equilibrium production model is central. This theory holds that there is the maximum economic yield (MEY), which occurs at the effort level yielding the greatest margin of revenue over cost from the resource. For a linear cost curve, this occurs to the left of MSY on the fishing effort axis. The total revenue curve (TR) has the same shape as the sustainable biological yield curve given in figure. TR depends upon the effort applied and the stock size.

The model being basically a static one, a constant price of fish for all quantities of fish and a constant cost per unit of fishing effort, are assumed. As effort increases total revenue from catch increases up to MSY but after that it declines. The reason is that as effort increases, the average yield per unit of effort falls because there are more fishermen fishing a declining stock. The marginal yield or the yield of the last unit of effort applied falls faster than the average yield. With increasing effort being applied to the fishery, total cost rises continually over time. The open access firms enter the industry until the economic rent is zero, that is where total revenue equals total cost. In Figure 6(b) "E" represents open access equilibrium, corresponding to fishing effort E3. A level of fishing above E3 would result in at least fishermen making losses and as a result they leave the fishery industry. Instead if effort is below E3, then fishermen earn excess profits and many more firms are induced to enter until profits are competed away. The profit-maximising equilibrium E does not coincide with MSY.

THE GORDON-SCHAEFER BIO-ECONOMIC EQUILIBRIUM MODEL

Problems associated with many fishing communities are that the opportunity cost of labour and capital devoted to fishing effort are low. Since few alternative employment opportunities exist, the resources get locked into fishing at high levels of effort. This situation is damaging to the sustainability of fish stocks. The bio-economic equilibrium represents economic over fishing where resources devoted to the fishing effort are more than the socially optimal requirement. The fishery may also show biological over fishing where the harvest is not below the MSY (Hanley *et al.* 1997, p. 287). In extreme cases this may lead to the fish population being reduced to such low levels that its exploitation is no longer viable. Markets will fail to reach efficient outcomes because of the non-excludability characteristics of the open access resource. Each fishermen has an incentive to maximize his catch, it is not rational for any individual fisherman to restrict his fishing effort, as there is no guarantee that he will receive any of the rewards in terms of catches later. In such circumstances each firm will exploit the fishery to its maximum potential, subject only to the constraint that its revenues must at least cover its costs.

The Gordon-Schaefer model neglects the dynamics of the economic and biological processes that govern a fishery. The basic assumptions of the model are highly restrictive. Fisheries tend to be highly variable, multi-species systems with biological and social dynamics which are overlooked in the stable single-species systems of bio-economic theory(Wilson, 1982, p. 147). These aspects are taken care of in comparative dynamic models of fishing. Comparative dynamics are concerned with the time

---

Note: MRR: Maximum Resource Rent.

path of the stock, how it is affected by market structure, policy measures and stock stability (Hanley et al. 1997, p-288). The sole ownership dynamic model is suitable for inland fisheries but it is unrealistic in the case of marine fisheries, but it defines the social optimum and provides insights for the formulation of fisheries policies.

In yet another modification of the Gordon-Schaefer model, biodiversity variables were introduced to make it applicable to the multi-species fishery. The model was then applied to the fresh water fishery in Lake Malawi (Kasulo and Perrings, 2000, p. 1). The aggregated multi-species Gordon-Schaefer model expresses the change in stock biomass as a difference between the aggregate of different species and the effect of the diversity of those species on the dynamics of the aggregated fishery. This model can be used to explain the importance of the level of diversity in a fishery in open access and profit maximizing regimes. In an open access situation, catches are maximized at higher levels of bio-economic diversity. Environmental factors like water pollution can affect fish diversity and productivity through eutrophication. The aggregated and modified Gordon-Schaefer model considers three different factors where environmental factors affect fish biomass. The first is through an effect on the carrying capacity, k, the second, through an effect on the intrinsic growth rate, r, and third through an effect on k and r together. Factors that affect recruitment and survival of fish stocks are assumed to affect the carrying capacity of the aquatic environment. Specifically, water pollution is assumed to have a negative effect on total fish bio-mass through its impact on food availability. Considering the afore mentioned factors the growth function for fish biomass takes the form

$$X = rx\,(1 - eW - X/k) - qEx$$

Where, W is the environmental quality variable and e is a parameter that gives the amount by which a unit change in the environmental variable depresses the natural growth of fish biomass. E represents fishing effort and X is fish stock. The introduction of biodiversity variable into the model captures the effects of biological as well as economic factors on the system. Unweighted and weighted biodiversity variables were developed for the purpose. The unweighted index assumes that all species are of equal values. The weighted index takes into account the different market values of species. Fish production depends not only on the level of effort and the size of the fish stock but also on the level of fish diversity. Usually fish stocks are exploited from more abundant to less abundant species, from easily caught to less easily caught species, and from high valued to less valued species. This requires the specification of an appropriate production function showing the relationship between fish diversity as an input and fish catch as an output.

Kasulo and Perrings assumed that the effects of species diversity on fish productivity may be captured by the introduction of an additional term into the fisheries production. The production function then becomes,

$$Y = qB\,Ex$$

Where, B is the economic diversity index when B=1, the production function reduces to the form in single species fishery models. If B<1, there is more than one economically valuable harvested species, the productivity of fishing effort tends to decline. The growth and sustainable yield functions change and take the following form

$$X= rx\,(1\text{-}eW - x/k) - q\,BEx$$

and

$$Y = qkBE\,(\,1\text{-}eW - qBE/r)$$

According to fishery scientists the pursuit of an economic efficiency criterion is not sufficient to guarantee the survival of fish resources in perpetuity. The concept of a safe minimum standard of conservation (SMC), has been advocated as a response to this set of circumstances (Perman et al. 1996, p-186). This would involve imposing constraints on resource harvesting and use so that all risks to the survival of the fish species are eliminated.

Resource exploitation in the case of marine fisheries has the adverse consequences of open access. One of the ways of dealing with this may be to define and allocate property right to the resource. Many nations have extended their limits of national jurisdiction to 200 miles over their coastal waters. But the access restriction must be enforceable. Many fish stocks within and outside EEZs are currently subject to ineffective management measures (FAO, 1994). The 1982 United Nations Convention on the law of the sea (UN 1983) is a key reference point for discussion on national and international fisheries management. International processes, including conferences, conventions and odes that are of significance to fisheries and coastal areas include the United Nations Convention on the Law of the Sea (UNCLOS, 1982), the United Nations Conference on Environment and Development (UNCED, 1992) and the consequent programme of Action, Agenda 21, the convention on Biological Diversity (CBD, 1992), the United Nations Agreement on Straddling Fish Stocks and Highly Migratory Fish Stocks (1993/94), the FAO's Code of Conduct for Responsible Fisheries(CCRF,1995) and the Regional Seas Conventions under the United Nations Environment Programme(UNEP, 1974). The International Convention for the Prevention of Pollution from ships (MARPOL, 73/78) and the London Dumping Convention (LDC, 1972). The CCRF, in its introductory chapter directs states and all those engaged in fisheries management to adopt measures for the long-term, conservation and sustainable use of fisheries resources.

Assessment of fisheries resources, in quantitative and qualitative terms, is an essential input for their optimum exploitation. Countries like New Zealand and Japan introduced an individual transferable quota system (ITQ) for their major fisheries. Government scientists annually assess fish stock levels, and determine total allowable catches (TAC). The TAC is then divided among fishers. Each fisher can catch fish up to the amount of the quota it holds, or the quotas can be sold or otherwise traded.

Fisheries policies of India, in the last five decades have accelerated the transformation of the traditional, subsistence-oriented marine fisheries into a market-oriented multi-crore industrial sector. The characteristic tropical species diversity is rich in Indian marine fisheries. There are nearly 1570 species of fin fishes and about 1000 species of shell fishes known from Indian seas. India's capture fisheries progressively increased from about 0.5 million tones in 1950 to 2.71 tones in 1997, showing an average annual growth of 6.4%. However, the growth rate declined from 6.5% during 1950-60 to 2.3% during 1960-70, increased to 4.3% during 1970-80 and to 4.8% during 1980-90 and declined to 4% during 1990-96 (CMFRI, 1998). The annual growth of capture fisheries has increased from 0.39% in 2001-02 to 0.72% in 2007-08. Fishing efforts largely confined to the inshore water through artisanal, traditional, mechanical sectors. About 90% of the present production from the marine sector is from with in a depth range of up to 50 to 70 meters and remaining 7% is contributed by deep seafishing fleets confining their operation mainly do the shrimp ground in the upper east coast.

CPR & AQUACULTURE

The rights of property, as such have not been venerated by those master minds who have built up economic science; but the authority of the science has been wrongly assumed by some who have pushed the claims of vested rights to extreme and antisocial uses. It may be well therefore to note that the tendency of careful economic study is to base the rights of private property not on any abstract principle, but on the observation that in the past they have been inseparable from economic progress. (Alfred Marshall).

It is a commonplace to observe that for natural resource-as for other types of wealth-"everybody's property is nobody's property". No one will take the trouble to husband and maintain a resource unless he has a reasonable certainty of receiving some portion of the product of his management; that is, unless he has some property rights in the yield. Yet the mere existence of the institution of private property is not sufficient to insure the efficient management of natural resources; the property must be allocated on a scale sufficient to insure that one management has complete control of the asset. For example, it is shown that private property in fishing boats is not a sufficient condition for efficiency; sole ownership of the fishery is also necessary. Some assets, such as oil fields, fisheries, and watersheds, occur on an immense scale, and it is a real problem to know whether the efficiency gained from unified management provides a social gain sufficient to offset the possible dangers of the creation of some immense sole ownership organization(such as a co-operative, a government board, a private corporation, or an International authority).

THE FISHERY: THE OBJECTIVES OF SOLE OWNERSHIP

In the central part of Gordan's paper, "The Bionomic Equilibrium of the Fishing Industry", he sets out to suggest the nature of the equilibrium of the common-property industry as it occurs in the state of uncontrolled or unmanaged exploitation. He undertakes to indicate the nature of a socially optimum manner of exploitation which is presumably what governmental management policy seeks to achieve or promote.

Gordan first argues that, because there is no sole owner to capture for himself whatever gain there may be from using the fishery conservatively, it will pay every fisherman to enter the industry so long as he can earn something above his cash expenses plus his opportunity costs. As long as fishermen do this, the tendency will be for exploitation to continue beyond the point where the marginal product of fishing effort equals its marginal costs, to the point where the average product of effort just covers the marginal cost of effort (where, in fact, every fisherman just covers his opportunity costs, and average cost is equal to price). There tends, it is argued, to be no "surplus" earned in the industry-the dollar value of the catch exactly equals the dollar cost of landing the catch.

Under such a regime, the argument continues, the possible equilibrium of effort, fish population, and income may be described in terms of a system of four variables, which may be drawn in four figures. These diagrams can be conveniently studied in one four–quadrant diagram.

If we start with the two upper quadrants, we see that output (or landings) L depends upon both the size of the input(or effort) E and the size of the capital stock, or population, P. The size of the capital stock, or population, is in turn itself

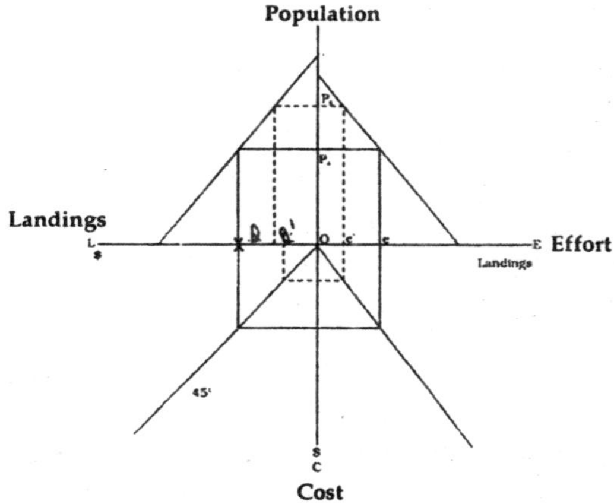

Figure 7

assumed to be dependent upon the effort. In the southeast quadrant is a cost function, C, showing constant marginal costs of effort, and in the southwest quadrant is a simple transition function of 45° which confronts the cost of various kinds of effort with the revenue from various sizes of landing. The condition of equilibrium is that the total costs must equal the total revenues O*l*. In diagrammatic terms there must be an inscribed rectangle in the four quadrants. Hence the dotted lines do not represent an equilibrium, but the solid lines do.

Assume that, in equilibrium, a certain total "effort", E (that is, of fishermen-plus-equipment), is being expended in the fishery. This effort, expended annually is compatible with a certain size of fish population, shown on the P-axis, and there is an equilibrium annual catch that can be achieved by this effort with this population, shown on the L-axis. But, as was argued above, the fishery will not be in equilibrium unless the cost of expending that effort (shown on C- axis) is exactly equal to the revenue, L. When L and C coincide, the fishery is in equilibrium.

A condition for achieving a positive, stable equilibrium is that there must be one and only one rectangle that will fit into the four quadrants. There may be no unique equilibrium possible, given the three functions, unless one of them is curvilinear, or (as here) unless the E- and L-functions have different intercepts on the P-axis. It is also possible to show the suggested equilibrium position of a sole owner. The dotted lines may now be used to represent this equilibrium: the difference at *l'* between the cost and the landings revenue is assumed to have been maximized Gordon's description of the equilibrium applies to this diagram:

Gordon calls these two situations "positions of equilibrium." It is true that in the first, the competitive exploitation of the fishery, the equilibrium indicates values of C, P and E that are compatible with one another, though we are not told just how the fisherman arrives at this equilibrium. It should be noted that it is quite possible that a competitive fishery in the process of production which might be described diagrammatically as a trial and error procedure of searching for the inscribed rectangle might easily miss an unstable equilibrium and gravitate rapidly between the alternate extremes of zero output and zero population. Furthermore, in those fisheries there may be no stable equilibrium short of zero landings and full natural population. It is not unlikely that fished-out lakes - which are, after all, demersal fisheries in the *economic* sense of Gordon's paper-would be examples of this impossibility of finding a competitive equilibrium position.

"Would be" because the fundamental assumption in Gordon's paper (apart from the admittedly unknown nature of the biological relationship between landings and demersal populations) is that there are in fishing no diminishing returns and hence no increasing costs and no incentive to stop operations short of the equality of total costs and landings. Surely this fundamental assumption is incorrect; surely in the short run (with population and equipment fixed) each fishing boat will experience increasing costs as it attempts to increase its landings.

Gordon's analysis, which has been followed in the above figure, relies upon the depletion of the population to produce a species of "diminishing returns" effect that will explain, with price given, why the competitive fishery does not expand indefinitely. But this explanation applies only to the long run and cannot hold within a single season, when the fish population is one of the fixed inputs. In the short run, fishermen do not expand their catch indefinitely because they do experience increasing costs in attempting to increase their landings. Gordon depends upon the omnibus variable "effort" to cover the changeable combinations of men, boats, and other equipment used by individual fishermen. But, if we look through this omnibus variable, we see that in fact the short-run situation in a fishery exploited by competing fishermen will be very like the standard situation in pure competition. The supply curve of this fishery (with the price given by the world market situation) will be made up by the addition of the relevant portions of the supply curves of the individual fishermen. These curves will slope upward because, with fixed equipment and a fixed number of boats, there will be some number of landings per boat which has a least cost; if the crew worked long hours, or the boat is kept running without time for maintenance or repair, the cost per landing will begin to rise. Each boat will increase its landings until its supply price (marginal cost) is equal to the going price. The "surplus" that might be captured in this situation is the usual quasi-rent, available to each boat by operating at the point where marginal costs are equal to marginal revenue.

Since the work of Ramsey, it has been clearly recognized that capital theory is in essence a problem in the calculus of variations. It was also recognized, however, that, in its classical formulation, the techniques provided by calculus of variations were inadequate to the task. The extensions of calculus of variations provided by optimal control theory eliminated the inadequacies of the classical techniques to a large extent. Economists were quick to appreciate the implications for capital theory; indeed, Dorfman goes so far as to argue that modern capital theory traces its origins to the development of optimal control theory. It seemed only a matter of time before the techniques of optimal control theory would be brought to bear upon fisheries economics.

Several attempts in this direction have by now been made. With the aid of a simple linear model most of the major results achieved so far have been summarized, but does so in a manner such that the links with capital theory are made transparent. Two sets of problems that have yet to be properly dealt with in the fisheries economics literature have also been explored. The first concerns the optimal approach to the equilibrium stock, i.e., the optimal "investment" policy. The second set of problems arises from the relaxation of the highly restrictive assumption of autonomy (i.e., the assumption that the parameters are independent of time). Conclusion is made with the examination of the complexities that can arise when the assumption of linearity is relaxed.

By assuming perfectly elastic demand, Gordon's analysis avoided consideration of consumers surplus in determining the socially optimum level of output of a fishery. In the following figure (Figure 8) that assumption has been relaxed.

In this case the output of the fishery concerned is not marginal to the market, so that any perceptible change in output will affect the amount of consumers surplus generated. With free entry the competitive equilibrium established in the fishery at A will result in an output of OB, generating a consumer's surplus of ACD. In this instance the market revenue

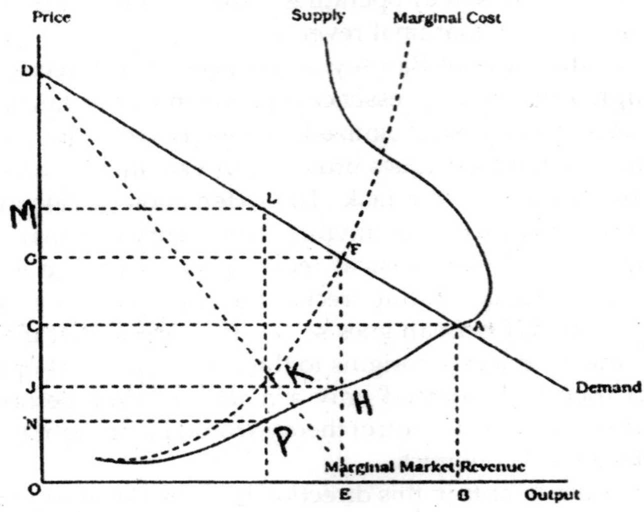

Figure 8

of the fishery (ABOC) is fully absorbed by social cost, which equals the private opportunity costs of fishing units. The consumer's surplus, being in excess of market revenue, and thereby in excess of social cost, represents a net social benefit. It is possible, however, to interpose between market revenue and the cost of employing fishing units a return to the resource in the form of rent, which would equally constitute a net social benefit. The socially optimum output, then, must maximize the combined total of rent and consumers surplus. The socially optimum output, of course, will be found at the point where marginal social cost and marginal social revenue are equal. In Figure 8 the supply curve has already been identified as an average social cost curve, with a matching marginal curve. The demand curve is a marginal social revenue curve, measuring as it does the addition to total social revenue for each additional unit of output. The socially optimum output now is found at F and maximum net social benefit is given by consumer's surplus (FGD) plus rent (FHJG). In moving from output OB to the optimal OE the price that will clear the market rises from OC to OG. This will bring with it a reduction in consumer's surplus, which is more than offset by the gain in rent. The latter could be acquired by the state in the form of production-related taxes or license fees (and possibly redistributed to consumers), or it could accrue to the group that is privileged to prosecute the restricted fishery.

The granting of sole ownership rights in respect of a fishery is often advocated as one way of approaching optimum exploitation. Whether the owner is the state or a private agency, it is argued, the owner would have an interest in maximizing the return from the fishery. The dissipation of rent by excessive effort that occurs with free entry could be prevented. The consideration of consumer's surplus, however, does raise the question whether a sole owner would be correctly motivated toward the achievement of a socially optimum level of exploitation. In particular, there may be a difference in the respective motivations of public and private agencies. A private firm, granted the sole right to exploit a fishery, presumably would have no interest in consumer's surplus. To such a firm the demand curve would not be a marginal revenue curve but an average revenue curve. A corresponding marginal (market) revenue curve may be determined. But as the private firm would have to pay for capital and labour inputs at the rate of the opportunity costs of marginal units, the supply curve would remain the average cost curve for the firm. The intersection of the marginal market revenue and marginal cost curves at K in Figure 2 shows the maximum rent obtainable by the private sole owner as LMNP. But maximizing rent and consumer's surplus together is bound to yield a greater net social benefit than maximizing rent alone (except where the demand curve is perfectly elastic, when consumers surplus will be zero). A public sole ownership agency, if instructed to observe marginal cost pricing, would operate at the socially optimum output level of OE, charging consumers a price of OG and maximizing the combined net social benefits of consumers' surplus (FGD) and rent (FHJG).

Turvey observed that the "maximum gain" that may be derived from the exploitation of a fishery contains three elements. Not only consumer's surplus and resource rent are involved, but also producers surplus. The latter consists of the rent that intra marginal inputs of labour and capital enjoy to the extent that their opportunity costs per unit of output lie below those of the marginal inputs of these factors. For to that extent intra-marginal factors inputs will receive revenue in excess of their opportunity costs; at least if there is no price discrimination and all factor inputs are remunerated according to the opportunity cost of the marginal inputs. In much of the theoretical literature of fisheries economics the consideration of producers surplus is avoided by assuming the equality of market cost and social cost and by assuming the equality of the cost of all units of fishing output. The consequences of the removal of these simplifying assumptions will now be explored.

Here are generally two reasons for which intra-marginal factor inputs may have opportunity costs below those of marginal factor inputs in a fishery. In the first place, differences in alternative employment and income opportunities for various fishermen and their gear may exist. But what is probably far more important is the difference in efficiency of various fishing units. To accommodate these phenomena in the model of this paper the following understanding is needed. Inputs of labour and capital will be considered combined into units of fishing effort of equal productive capacity. Such units of fishing effort then will be equal in terms of amount of catch produced, but not necessarily in terms of amount of equipment used, numbers of crew members employed, extent of fishing time or level of operating cost. Translated into a practical example this means that if one vessel-crew combination produces twice as much fish as another, the former will be considered to represent two units of fishing effort as against one unit for the latter. This will be so even where the vessels would be identical physically and have equal numbers of crew members with individually equal opportunity costs, equal hours of fishing time and equal operating expenses. In such a case the opportunity costs in absolute terms for the two vessel-crew combinations would be the same. But for the former vessel they would be distributed over two units of fishing effort and would therefore be shown at half the level of the opportunity costs for the one unit of fishing effort represented by the latter vessel.

In his leading article Gordon remarked: "By and large, the only fisherman who becomes rich is one who makes a lucky catch or one who participates in a fishery that is put under a form of social control that turns the open resource into property rights". This notion has confirmed economists in their belief that they have found the explanation of this poverty in the peculiar common property nature of the fishery that leads to the dissipation of the resource rent. But the economists' notion is challenged by many practical men in the fishing business who know that significant numbers of fishermen and fishing company operators earn large incomes and that some gain small fortunes. They also know that the high earners, who operate competitively in fisheries with unrestricted entry, do not depend on luck, but perform consistently at much higher levels of efficiency than do their rivals.

The difference in a fishery between marginal opportunity costs, which match revenue, and the lower opportunity costs of intra-marginal fishing units is a form of rent (or quasi rent). This rent is the substance of the producer's surplus. It is not attributable to the nature of the resource as such, but is primarily related to the efficiency of the intra marginal fishing units. Nevertheless, this rent must be considered a feature of the fishery as the efficiency from which it derives is an efficiency of labour and capital that is peculiar to their specific application to the fishery resource. The same units of labour and capital may or may not have any efficiency advantage in alternative employment. A good fisherman may not be any good at any other trade. The notion that fisheries allowing free entry yield no rent therefore requires qualification, for considerable rents may be earned by intra-marginal factor units specifically as a result of their employment in the fishery. The literature of fisheries economics has tended to ignore the significance of this rent, perhaps because it was thought of as a matter of small differences in terms of alternative employment opportunities instead of large differences in terms of operational efficiency.

The introduction of producer's surplus into the analysis requires the differentiation of social cost from market cost. This is illustrated in Figure 9.

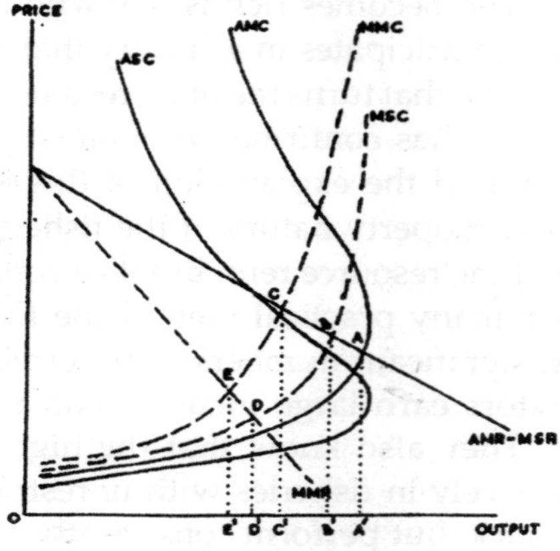

Figure 9

The AMC curve represents the supply curve. It measures the average market cost at each output level as determined by the opportunity costs of marginal units of fishing effort. For a competitive fishery this is the operational long-run supply curve that will indicate output equilibrium for various price levels. The MMC (marginal market cost) curve has been drawn marginal to the AMC curve. It measures marginal cost per unit of output to any operator possessing sole ownership rights in respect of the fishery resource (e.g., a state fishing monopoly or a private fishing company with an exclusive licence), but hiring other factors (labour and capital) at rates determined by the marginal opportunity cost of fishing effort. The ASC (average social cost) curve is obtained by subtracting the average producers surplus from the average market cost and thus represents the average opportunity cost per unit of output for labour and capital. The MSC (marginal social cost) curve is drawn marginal to the ASC curve. Also in Figure 9 a demand curve is shown. It functions both as an average market revenue (AMR) curve and a marginal social revenue (MSR) curve, in so far as it measures at any output the additional value enjoyed by consumers at the price the marginal buyer is prepared to pay. A marginal market revenue (MMR) curve has been drawn marginal to the demand curve to show the marginal revenue enjoyed by sellers collectively (or by a monopoly seller) for the output of the fishery.

Figure 9 may now be used to identify the different equilibrium positions that relate to control over the fishery resource by various interest groups. Generally, three distinctly different interest groups may be recognized. Consumers would benefit from a regime that would maximize consumers' surplus. Private owners of the fishery resource would want to maximize resource rent. Finally, the owners of other factors (labour and capital) would profit from the maximization of their factor rents in the form of producers surplus. Maximizing equilibrium positions are identified by the intersection of appropriate marginal revenue and marginal cost schedules. Having identified two marginal revenue and two marginal cost schedules, the permutations permit four distinct equilibrium positions. Three of these represent, in turn, the primacy of each one of the three interest groups, while the fourth represents the optimum position of social control in the joint interest. There is also a fifth equilibrium position that is non-maximizing. It results from the free interplay of market forces. Major characteristics of these five positions have been summarized in the table while Figure 10 illustrates graphically the relationship of the three categories of social benefits in each equilibrium position. Further comment on the five equilibrium positions follows:

(A) The intersection of the market demand and supply curves produces an equilibrium output OA^1 that will apply in an open entry fishery supplying a competitive market. This is the laissez-faire position that is approached in most common property fisheries. It results in the dissipation of rent through over fishing, but allows for incidental amounts of consumers and producers surplus. Price and output equilibria may be above or below the socially optimum levels, depending in part on whether the equilibrium is located on the forward or backward slope of the supply curve.

(B) In terms of the definitions and assumptions, the socially optimum equilibrium position is given by the intersection of the marginal social revenue and marginal social cost curves at point B in Figure 9. This position allows for the largest total net social benefit by maximizing the combined total of consumers surplus, resource rent and producers surplus. It requires centralized control (presumably by government) to limit output to OB by holding fishing effort to the level determined by point P on the supply curve, as shown in Figure 10. The price charged to consumers will be B while options remain open for disposition of the rent.

(C) If consumers by collective action would acquire monopoly control over the market for the output of a fishery, they would be in a position to capture the rent available from the resource. They could then maximize the combined total of consumers surplus and rent to their own advantage. In this category one could think of a consumers co-operative as a monopsonist purchasing the entire catch from a group of competing fishermen. The optimum output for the monopsonist co-operative would be determined by the intersection of the MSR and MMC curves, shown at C in Figure 10(C). The monopsonist concerned with maximizing consumers benefits would be guided by the marginal social revenue schedule that relates to values enjoyed by consumers, rather than by the marginal market revenue schedule that would relate to money receipts by producers. Conversely, its unconcern for the welfare of producers would cause it to be guided by marginal market cost that relates to the cost of its purchases, rather than by the marginal social cost that relates to the opportunity costs of producers. To appropriate the resource rent the co-operative would have to use its monopsonist power to hold its buying price down to the opportunity cost of marginal fishing units as measured by QC. It would then capture a rent of QC per unit of product. An incidental amount of producer's surplus would still accrue to intramarginal fishing units. In disposing of the rent, the co-operative would have to avoid paying dividends to its members in proportion to the amount of fish purchased by these members. For this would effectively lower the price of fish to members, causing them to increase purchases. The culmination of this process would be the establishment of equilibrium at A in the free market position where rent would be dissipated. The co-operative would thus lose the advantage of its monopsonist position and the total benefits accruing to it and its members would diminish. If the co-operative were confronted in the market not by a number of competing fishermen, but by a monopolist seller, the division of the rent between monopsonist buyer and monopolist seller, the division of the rent between monopsonist buyer and monopolist seller would be indeterminate. Another example of a monopsonist buyer maximizing consumers' surplus plus resource rent could be a government marketing monopoly selling fish in a national market and contracting with foreign operators to deliver the fish. The government, presumably, would have an interest in capturing a maximum of consumers' surplus and rent for its citizens, but would have no interest in the foreign producers surplus.

(D) The case of the producer's monopoly is symmetrical to that of the consumer's monopsony. A co-operative or marketing association of all operators in a fishery (or a single operator representing all inputs in a fishery), when facing a multiplicity of buyers, could appropriate both resource rent and producers surplus. The optimum position for the producer's monopoly as indicated in Figure 10 (D), would be determined by the intersection of the MSC and MMR curves at D. The monopolist's concern for producer's incomes would be guided by the marginal social cost schedule that is related to the opportunity costs of producers. But on the sales side the marginal market revenue schedule would give the appropriate guidance, demonstrating unconcern for the social revenue of consumers. The monopolist seller would want to set the price at RD to appropriate a rent of RS per unit of product. This would maximize the resource rent and producers surplus accruing to the producer's monopoly, while leaving an incidental amount of consumer's surplus.

(E) The final case to be considered is that of sole ownership of a fishery resource where ownership is divorced from both consumer interest and the interests of other producing factors, i.e., capital and labour. One could think of a landowner (water owner in this case) renting the right to exploit a fishpond or oyster bed. The resource owner, in charging the maximum rent for which he can find takers, will cause an equilibrium output to be established at the level for which marginal market revenue and cost coincide. This is shown at point E in Figure 10(E). Incidental amounts of consumer's surplus and producer's surplus will accrue. Marginal operators will find that they can just cover their opportunity costs of TE per unit of output by charging the market price of UE and meeting the rent payment of UT per unit of output.

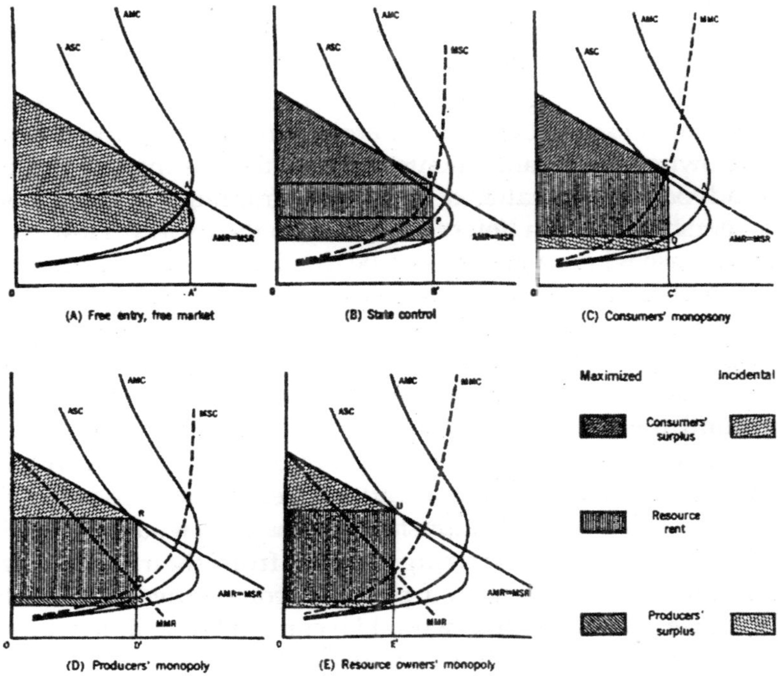

Figure 10

There are some common features of the three cases of private sole ownership or control of the resource i.e., cases (C), (D), and (E) when contrasted with case (B), which represents social control in the general interest. The private sole ownership arrangements all result in higher prices and lower outputs. They represent cases of under fishing. Indeed, a restriction of output is what one would expect in monopoly situations. In each of these cases only one or two of the three categories of social benefit are maximized, so that the total net social benefit achieved is less than that of the full social control case. Socially the least profitable is the case of the private resource owners' monopoly, which maximizes only one category of social benefit, viz., resource rent. Of the four cases it provides for the lowest output and the highest price.

It is clear that the equilibrium position in the competitive market with free entry to the fishery will be non-optimal. Resource rent will be dissipated. But there is nothing in the analysis to suggest that the incidental accretions of consumers and producers surplus in this case could not be in excess of the total net social benefits generated under any of the private sole ownership arrangements. A priori there is then no reason to advocate as a matter of policy the granting of private sole ownership rights in lieu of free entry to the fishery. However, in the case where a fishery can be divided into a large number of small fishing grounds that are not interacting biologically (perhaps in an oyster fishery), separate sole ownership rights might be given in respect of individual grounds. Owner-operators would have an interest in maximizing on each ground the producer's surplus plus rent. If they were then competing with the sale of their output in a perfectly competitive market, they would not detract from consumer's surplus. Under these circumstances fishermen would resemble wheat farmers, maximizing returns from their individual holdings while selling in a perfectly competitive market. In that case sole ownership would be compatible with the social optimum and would thus be superior to free entry.

VALUING MANGROVE-FISHERY LINKAGES

Shocked by ecologists' attempts to value wetland services (Gosselink et al. 1974), economists have spent over twenty-five years refining methods and estimated values (e.g. Barbier 1994; Batie and Wilson 1978; Bell 1989; Hammack and Brown 1974; Lynne et al. 1981; Shabman and Bertelson 1979; Turner 1991). There have even been joint efforts by the disciplines to determine wetland and estuarine system values (Farber and Costanza 1987; Kahn and Kemp 1985). In the process, the exchange of economic and ecological concepts has likely improved our knowledge of the contributions that wetlands make to our well-being.

One component of wetland valuation methodology, valuing the effects of wetlands on the flow of output from commercial fisheries, may have overlooked a fundamental characteristic of many fisheries: open access. Although most studies appreciate the necessity of controlling human effort while assessing the marginal productivity of wetlands, the fishery is generally not modeled in a framework that reflects the characteristics of open access. Here it is presented as a model which allows the vagaries of open access fishing to be considered, albeit crudely. In addition, we establish a value for one of the non-market functions of mangroves by exploring the relationship between mangroves and shrimp production in the State of Campeche, Mexico. Other fish species are also dependent on the mangroves, but the focus is on shrimp because it is critical to the region, its production is likely to be separable from the rest of the area's fishing, and its data are available. However, by focusing solely on shrimp, we obtain only a partial accounting of the entire indirect use value of the mangroves.

If the mangrove area in the Laguna de Terminos can be linked empirically to the production of shrimp, then there is evidence that mangrove depletion can have a deleterious effect on the shrimp industry and the entire Campeche economy. This evidence is especially important because the low price of mangrove areas is leading to their conversion to other than natural uses. In particular, the expansion of the city of Carmen, adjacent to Laguna de Terminos, has depleted the acreage of mangroves by more than 2% in the last decade. There is also concern that lucrative shrimp aquaculture activities will begin encroaching on the mangrove areas.

In addition, by attempting to value the contribution of the Laguna de Terminos mangrove system to the commercial shrimp fisheries of Campeche, this paper aims to develop a general methodology for valuing mangrove-fishery linkages that can be applied to mangrove and coastal wetland systems elsewhere. This approach is also consistent with other attempts to assess the economic value of coastal wetland habitats in support of marine fisheries and other ecological functions, such as determining the value of marshlands as habitat for Gulf Coast fisheries in the southern United States (Bell 1989, 1997; Ellis and Fisher 1987; Farber and Costanza 1987; Freeman 1991; Lynne *et al.* 1981), analyzing the competition between mangroves and shrimp aquaculture in Ecuador (Parks and Bonifaz 1994), determining the value of a multiple-use mangrove system under different management options in Bintuni Bay, Irian Jaya, Indonesia (Rluitenbeek 1994), and examining general coastal system trade-offs, such as the effects of development on habitat-fishery linkages (Kahn and Kemp 1985; Swallow 1990, 1994; Strand and Bockstael 1990; Suthawan 1997). In contrast to many of these approaches, however, we attempt to value wetland-fishery linkages through a straightforward adaptation of the standard open access bioeconomic model to incorporate changes in habitat area, in this case mangroves.

THE OPEN ACCESS EQUILIBRIUM

The analysis of fishery-mangrove linkages is conducted by examining the effects of a change in mangrove area on the long-run open access equilibrium of the Campeche shrimp fishery. In equilibrium, both the shrimp stock and the level of fishing effort are assumed to be constant over time, i.e. $X_{t+1} = X_t = X$ and $E_{t+1} = E_t = E$. In addition, it is assumed initially that the mangrove area is in equilibrium, i.e. $M_t = M_{t+1} = M$. For steady state equilibrium levels of shrimp stocks X, and effort E, the equation will be thus;

$$X=c/pq, \text{ for } E_{t+1}=E_t=E, \quad (1)$$

The Equilirium is shown in Figure below:

$$E = r(K(M)-X)/q, \text{ for } X_{t+1} + X_t=X. \quad (2)$$

Equation (1) is the standard open access condition that assumes any profits in the fishery will be competed away in the long run. Equation (2) indicates the combinations of fishing effort

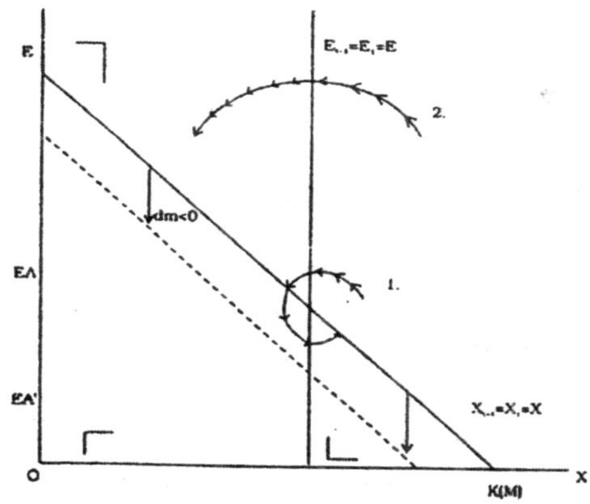

Figure 11

and shrimp stock size (and thus also mangrove area) that will lead to a constant level of shrimp stock in the fishery in the long run. Figure 10 depicts the equilibrium conditions in (X,E) space. The $E_{t+1}=E_t = E$ curve is of course vertical, given Equation (1). From Equation (2) the slope of the $X_{t+1} = X_t = X$ curve in (X,E) space is downward sloping, i.e. $dE/dX = -r/q<0$.

Two possible trajectories for fishing effort and shrimp stocks are depicted in Figure 10, assuming an initial level of stock Xo. Trajectory 1 is essentially a stable spiral that leads to open access equilibrium denoted by $(X^{A'}, E^A)$. Trajectory 2 leads to rapid decline of the shrimp fishery from the outset to near extinction or 'collapse' levels, which, as depicted, could occur if the initial level of effort is too high, given Xo.

As shown in Figure 10, because the mangrove area affects the carrying capacity of the shrimp fishery, the impact of mangrove deforestation on the system represented by Equations (1) and (2) is to shift down the $X_{t+1} = X_t = X$ curve. This results in a lower steady-state level of effort, E^{A1}, although equilibrium stock is unchanged. Assuming that a trajectory to this new equilibrium is still feasible given the initial stock Xo, then the impacts of mangrove loss on carrying capacity will also mean a lower level of initial fishing effort. Thus in the model of mangrove-fishery linkages, the open access fishery adjusts to the impacts of mangrove loss by reducing both initial and equilibrium levels of effort. If the fishery fails to do this, then it may instead find on a different exploitation path, such as trajectory 2, that leads to 'near collapse' of shrimp stocks.

In the analysis, it is estimated that the impacts of mangrove deforestation on the stable open access equilibrium assuming that fishery effort adjusts instantaneously to allow a new equilibrium to be attained. We do not consider the case where the effect of deforestation is to make a steady-state equilibrium infeasible, thus causing the shrimp fishery to switch to a different exploitation path, such as that represented by trajectory 2 in Figure. As discussed above, there is evidence that mangrove deforestation in Laguna de Terminos is affecting the Campeche shrimp fishery, but it is unlikely that the fishery is currently in danger of the 'near collapse' scenario depicted by trajectory 2. Thus in the following analysis of the effect of a change in mangrove area, it is assumed that the fishery has attained a stable open access equilibrium, such as the steady-state (X^A, E^A) depicted in Figure 10, and therefore it is analyzed the impacts of mangrove deforestation on the fishery in terms of changes in the equilibrium steady-state conditions.

THE COMPARATIVE STATIC EFFECTS OF A CHANGE IN MANGROVE AREA

For simplicity, it is assumed a proportional relationship between mangrove area and carrying capacity, i.e. let K(M) = aM, a > 0. Thus, from equation (2), the comparative static effect of a change in the mangrove area on the equilibrium level of fishing effort, E^A is

$$r[\alpha dM - dX^A] - qdE^A$$

(or)

$$dE^A/dM = ar/q > 0. \tag{3}$$

This confirms that loss of the mangrove area results in a lower level of equilibrium fishing effort. From the equation, $h_t = q\,X_t\,E_t$(the basic Schaefer production process for harvesting h_t) it is clear that there will be a loss of harvest as well. Utilizing equation (3) and (1), the impact on the equilibrium harvest level can be solved for explicitly

$$dh^A = qX^A dE^A = \alpha r X^A dM = \alpha rc/pq\ dM > 0 \quad (4)$$

The resulting change in gross revenue of the fishery is then

$$pdh^A = \alpha rc/q\ dM > 0 \quad (5)$$

A fall in the mangrove area will therefore result in a decline in both steady-state shrimp harvest and the gross revenue of the fishery. Moreover, given that these impacts are based on the bioeconomic parameters of the model (α, r and q) combined with prices and costs for the fishery (p and c), it is possibly to estimate these comparative static effects explicitly.

EMPIRICAL ESTIMATION OF MANGROVE-FISHERY LINKAGES

By employing one of the above equilibrium conditions of the model, it is possible to establish a relationship between shrimp production, effort and mangrove area that can be estimated over time. This regression is run utilizing the Campeche shrimp fishery and mangrove area data over the 1980-90 period. The resulting parameter estimates allows to determine the appropriate combination of α,r, and q that underly the comparative static results of the model. By also incorporating values for the economic parameters p and c, it is possible to simulate the comparative static effects of a change in mangrove area on equilibrium harvest and gross revenue of the shrimp fishery over the 1980-90 period of analysis.

If it is assumed in the analysis that the shrimp stock is constant, i.e. $X_t = X_{t+1} = X$, then the steady-state condition (2) to derive a relationship between shrimp production, mangrove area and effort. By substituting equation (2) into equation (6) and re-arranging, we obtain.

$$h = qEK(M) - q^2/r\ E^2 = qaEM - q^2/r\ E^2 \quad (6)$$

Equation (6) can be estimated by employing the available time series data over 1980-90 on shrimp harvests, effort and mangrove area for Campeche, Mexico. By assuming that it would take 5.5 artisanal boats on average to harvest the same amount as an industrial boat, we can combine the data on the number of artisanal and industrial boats in the Campeche fishing industry to form a composite effort variable E. In Equation (6) h is represented as annual harvest in kilograms (kg) of shrimp by both artisanal and industrial boats, M is the annual mangrove area (sq km) in Laguna de Terminos and E is the composite, or aggregate, harvesting effort each year. We estimate this equation over the period 1980-90, the years for which data are available, and assume that any resulting error term is identically independently distributed over time. A summary of the results is presented in the Table 1. Except for not being able to reject autocorrelation (test is inconclusive), the regression results and the co-efficient estimates are quite good and were fairly robust for slightly different specifications of the model.

The marginal productivity and output elasticity estimates corresponding to the regression of equation (6) are also shown in Table 1. Calculated using the mean level of effort (5556 combined vessels), the marginal productivity of mangrove area is 24.7 metric tons per km². This is because MP_M is proportional to the level of effort, and over the 1980-90 period the number of vessels in the Campeche shrimp fishery increased substantially, from around 4500 combined vessels in 1980 to over 7200 in 1990. In contrast, the marginal productivity of fishing effort (calculated at mean effort and mean mangrove area, 849 km²) is actually negative in the regression, at an average of –0.997 tons per vessel. MPE was slightly negative in 1980, at –26 kg per vessel, but fell to –2.48 tons per vessel by 1990. Part of this decline in the marginal productivity of effort is due to the loss in mangrove area in the Laguna de Terminos from 1980 to 1990, but by far the more important influence appears again to be the increase in the number of small fishing vessels over this period.

The output elasticity for the mangrove area (2.80) indicates that a decline in the Laguna de Terminos mangroves has a more than proportionate impact on output in the Campeche shrimp fishery. However, the overall impact of mangrove loss during the 1980-90 periods on the fishery was still relatively small. Only 2.3% of the mangrove area was deforested between 1980 and 1990, which would suggest that the corresponding loss in fishery output was around 6.5%. The negative output elasticity for effort (-0.74) indicates that the increase in fishing effort over the 1980-90 period had a significant negative impact on shrimp production. As the number of combined vessels increased by

Table 1
Characteristics of Equilibrium Levels of Output and Price for Different Forms of Fisheries Management

Market organization	*Categories of benefits maximized*	*Incidental social benefits*	*Social benefits eliminated*	*Relation to socially optimum output*	*Relation of consumers' price to social optimum*	*Relation to socially optimum level of effort*
(A) Free entry and free market	—	Consumers' surplus and producers' surplus	Resource rent	Indeterminate	Indeterminate	Overfishing
(B) State· control	Combined total of consumers' surplus, resource rent and producers' surplus	—	—	Optimal	Optimal	Optimal
(C) Consumers' monopsony	Combined total of consumers' surplus and resource rent	Producers' surplus	—	Below optimum	Above optimum	Underfishing
(D) Producers' monopoly	Combined total of producers' surplus and resource rent	Consumers' surplus	—	Below optimum	Above optimum	Underfishing
(E) Resource owners' monopoly	Resource rent	Consumers' surplus and producers' surplus	—	Below optimum	Above optimum	Underfishing

61.5% over this period, the corresponding loss in shrimp harvest was 45.5%.

As it yields only two coefficient estimates, the regression of equation (6) is insufficient to determine explicitly the three-bioeconomic parameters (α,r, and q). However, it is not necessary to solve for the values of these three parameters in order to estimate the comparative static relationships equation (4) and (5). For example, denoting the estimated coefficients of Equation (6) as b_1=aq and $b_2=-q^2/r$, it follows that equation (4) and (5) can be rewritten as

$$dh^A = \alpha rc/pq\ dM = -cb_1/pb_2\ dM,\alpha \quad (4')$$

$$pdh^A = arc/q\ dM = -cb_1/b_2\ dM. \quad (5')$$

Thus to determine the comparative static effects (4′) and (5′) requires imputing values for prices and costs p and c and combining these values with the parameter estimates b_1 and b_2 from our regression of Equation (6). We impute values to p and c through the following approach.

As noted above, the assumption underlying the estimation of Equation (6) is that the 1980-90 shrimp harvest and effort data for the Campeche fishery satisfy one of the open access equilibrium conditions of our model, i.e. Equation (2). However, the latter is only one of the conditions necessary for open access equilibrium. The other is Equation (1), which assumes zero profits in the long run. Values of h and E that satisfy both equation (6) and the long run zero profit condition will therefore also satisfy the open access equilibrium.

For the purposes of illustrating the comparative static effects of a change in the mangrove area on equilibrium harvest and revenues, it would be convenient to assume that the 1980-90 harvest and effort levels satisfy simultaneously both open access conditions, equations (1) and (2). This will be the case if the price and cost parameters in each of the years of data attain levels that equate with zero profits, i.e. ph=cE. Price data in terms of US$/kg of imported fresh/frozen shrimp from Mexico are available for the 1980-90 period. Assuming a 100% mark-up from the ex-vessel prices, we use these data to generate a price series for the Campeche shrimp fishery. Consequently, based on the price, effort and harvest data, we calculate for each year of the analysis the corresponding 'equilibrium' cost per unit effort levels that yield zero profits, and denote these cost values as cA. Thus by employing our estimated parameters, b_1 and b_2, and the economic parameters, p and c^A, we are able to calculate the comparative static effects of the impacts of mangrove loss over 1980-90 on the open access Campeche shrimp fishery, as indicated by conditions (4') and (5').

On average over the 1980-90 period, a marginal (in km^2) decline in mangrove area produces a loss of 14.39 metric tons of shrimp harvest and US$139352 in revenues from the Campeche fishery each year. This is equivalent to a reduction of 0.19% in the annual harvest and revenues of the fishery. Since over the simulation period mangrove deforestation occurred at the rate of around 2 km^2 annually, the resulting loss each year amounts to about 28.8 metric tons, or US$278704. As our theoretical analysis would suggest, mangrove conversion in the Laguna de Terminos clearly has a negative impact on the Campeche shrimp fishery. However, given the relatively small rate of annual mangrove deforestation in the Laguna de Terminos over the 1980-90 period, the resulting loss in shrimp harvest and revenues does not appear to have been substantial. If, as expected, mangrove deforestation accelerates in the region, perhaps as a result of urban expansion and the conversion of mangrove swamps to Mari culture ponds, then it is likely that more substantial losses to the off-shore shrimp fishery will occur.

An interesting feature of our simulation is that it indicates how the economic losses associated with mangrove deforestation are affected by long-run management of the open access fishery. As noted previously, the early years of the period (e.g. 1980-81) were characterized by much lower levels of fishing effort and higher harvests (e.g. on average around 4800 combined vessels extracting about 8.5 KMT annually). If this earlier period represented the open access equilibrium of the fishery, the economic impacts of a marginal (km^2) decline in the mangrove area would be a reduction in annual shrimp harvests of around 18.6 tons, or a loss of about US$153300 per year. In contrast, the last two years of analysis (e.g. 1989-90) saw much higher levels of effort and lower harvests in the fishery (e.g. around 6700 combined vessels extracting 5.3 KMT annually). As a consequence, if this latter period represents the open access equilibrium, then a marginal decline in mangrove area would result in annual losses in shrimp harvests of 8.4 tons, or US$86345 each year.

Thus, the value of the Laguna de Terminos mangrove habitat in supporting the Campeche shrimp fishery appears to be affected by the level of exploitation. This suggests that, if an open access fishery is more heavily exploited in the long run, the subsequent welfare losses associated with the destruction of natural habitat supporting this fishery are likely to be lower. Intuitively, this makes sense. The economic value of an over-exploited fishery will be lower than if it were less heavily depleted in the long run. The share of this value that is attributable to the ecological support function of natural habitat will therefore also be smaller.

RENEWABLE NATURAL RESOURCES

The natural resource upon which mankind depends are of two classes. In one class are those resources, such, for example, as fossil fuels, mineral deposits, and elements capable of yielding energy by the conversion of mass to energy by nuclear processes, which are non-renewable, or for which the rate of renewal is so slow that it is infinitesimal compared to the rate of use. To this class of resources the concept of indefinitely sustainable yield cannot be applied. Man can use these resources rapidly or slowly, efficiently or inefficiently, but the total quantity on this planet is limited and is subject to being completely used up in finite time. In the second category are those resources which are constantly renewed, and are, therefore, capable of yielding sustained production indefinitely.

The different nature of renewable and non-renewable resources was clearly distinguished by Marshall (p. 166-167). Among the renewable resources there are, again two types with fundamental differences, those for which the rate of renewal is dependent on the amount of the resources which is left unharvested to perpetuate itself, and those where such dependence does not exist, or is negligible.

NON-SELF REGULATING RESOURCES

For the second type, which may be called non-self regulating resources, the amount which is available to be used each year is determined by natural phenomena other than the magnitude of the resource itself, and the amount which is used during a given year has no effect on the amount which will be available for use during the next year. The renewal of resources of this type is consequently independent of the rate of use. The concept of "land" as one of the factors of production in classical economic science is apparently based on the idealization of this type of resource. The concept is summarized by Marshall (p. 144):

"While man has no power of creating matter, he creates utilities by putting things into a useful form; and the utilities made by him can be increased in supply if there is an increased demand for them: they have a supply price. But there are other utilities over the supply of which he has no control; they are given as a fixed quantity by nature and have therefore no supply price. The term "land" has been extended by economists so as to include the permanent sources of these utilities; whether they are found in land as the term is commonly used, or in the seas and rivers, in sunshine and rain, in winds and waterfalls".

Renewable resources, by definition possess self-regeneration capacities and can provide man with an essentially endless supply of goods and services. But man, in turn, possesses capacities both for the conservation and for the destruction of the renewable resources base.

Indeed, man's increasing capacity to seriously deplete the world's natural resources appears to be reaching a critical stage (1)if this is not imminent for the nonrenewable resources (2) it certainly appears so for many of the renewable ones (3).The problems of environmental pollution that loom so large today, for example, often result from a process of overexploitation of the regenerative capacity of our atmospheric and water resources. Economists lately have devoted much attention to environmental questions.(4) and most agree that "externalities"– that is, effects not normally accounted for in the cost revenue analyses of producers–are the leading economic cause of pollution and the destruction of natural beauty. Animate resource, or biological resources, is also subject to serious misuse by man. An accelerating decline has been observed in recent years in the productivity of many important fisheries (5), particularly the great whale fisheries and the famous Grand Banks fisheries of the western Atlantic, as well as the spectacularly productive Peruvian anchovy fisheries (6). As technology improves and demand increases so the pressure on renewable resources grows more severe. The long-recognized need for effective international regulation of fisheries has never been so pressing as it is today. A prerequisite for effective regulation is a clear understanding of the basic reasons for overexploitation, and in this regard the outstanding articles by Hardin (7) on "The tragedy of the common" has been a positive asset, even though economists have long been aware of the common property problem in fisheries (8), Indeed, in concentrating their attention in the problems of competitive overexploitation of fisheries, economists appear to have a largely overlooked fact that a corporate owner of property rights. in a biological resources might actually prefer extermination to conservation, on the basis of maximization of profits (9). Over exploitation, perhaps even to the point of actual extinction, is a definite possibility under private management of renewable resources.

Exploitation of renewable resources such as fish stocks shared by a limited number of agents involves strategic choices. Should the agents cooperate and maximize their aggregate returns, or is cooperation a futile exercise undertaken by the naïve, who will be outsmarted by the realistic? There exists by now a voluminous literature on this subject. Much of this literature was inspired by the international disputes over fishing limits in the 1970's and the deliberations of the third United Nations conference on the Law of the Sea 1973-1982 which endorsed the 200 mile exclusive economic zone. The two early papers in this genre are Munro (11) and Levhari and Mirman (9). Recently Fisher and Mirman (2,3) have extended the analysis to interacting species. Three of these papers compare Nash equilibria and global optima while Munro is concerned with bargaining solutions in cooperative games. All these papers deal with the case of two agents, which is true of most of the literature on game theory and fisheries; few authors have considered explicitly the importance of the number of agents for obtaining a cooperative solution. An exception is Clark (1) who does not, however, consider the implications of threat strategies in repeated games. Hamalainen *et al.*(6) do so, but again limit themselves to the case of two agents.

In 1982, the United Nations (U.N) Third Conference on the Law of the Sea closed and formally ushered in a new era in world fisheries management through the Law of Sea Convention (United Nations 1982). Under the Convention, coastal states throughout the world were enabled to extend their management jurisdiction over fishery resources from 12 to 200 (22.2 to 370.4 km) national miles. It was estimated that 90% of the harvest of marine fishery resources would be accounted for by resources encompassed by the coastal state 200 – mile (370.4-Km) zones-exclusive Economic Zones (EEZS; Kaitala and Munro 1995). The objective in establishing the EEZ regimes was to enhance the conservation and economic management of world marine fishery resources. In 1989, a Food and Agricultural Organization of the United Nations (FAO) publication, in anticipation of EEZ regime, stated that: "the opportunity exists, as never before, for the rational exploitation of marine fisheries... The 1980's provide the threshold for a new era in the enjoyment of the ocean's wealth in fisheries" (cited in United Nations Food and Agriculture Organization 1992).

GUIDELINES FOR "RESPONSIBLE" RENEWABLE RESOURCE POLICIES

Howe(1979) developed a set of six principles for responsible natural resources policy. They encompassed both exhaustible and renewable resources, but two are particularly useful for developing renewable resources policies.

1. The avoidance of irreversibilities in all renewable resource systems. Howe advocates using a safe minimum standard(SMS) approach, which he says must be defined specifically for each renewable resource system. A SMS for a unique natural system, Yellowstone Park, for example, might be defined as a minimum contiguous area needed to permit natural perpetuation of the system.
2. A clear determination of the role of free markets and prices. When Howe wrote his principles in 1979, he said that "current practice consists of a bad mixture of attempts at public control and partial reliance on private markets"(p. 336). Atmost two decades later, current practice remains glaringly similar. Market prices should be allowed to define actual conditions of scarcity. Subsidies that encourage destructive practices should be eliminated.

Regulation should provide market signals wherever possible to encourage efficient behaviour. The legacy of failed fisheries regulations that attempted to suppress technological innovation and artificially raise harvest costs should not be forgotten. Better to allow harvest to be done as efficiently as possible, but ensure that the total harvest is limited, in the same way that tradable pollution permits ensure a ceiling on overall pollution levels, but allow those levels to be achieved at the lowest possible cost.

DETERMINING OPTIMAL HARVESTING RATES

To examine optimal harvesting rates for a self-renewing biological resource, we begin with a typical growth curve. At low levels of biomass, the stock will increase at an increasing rate over time. When biomass is low, as with a stand of young trees or a thinned-out population of trees or fish, the growth rate is low because either there are too few individuals to capture all the resources available for growth (eg; light, nutrients), there is a low reproductive rate, or both. At some point, however, the rate of increase will begin falling until eventually a maximum level of the stock will be reached. This maximum stock value sometimes is called the carrying capacity (Pearce and Turner 1990).

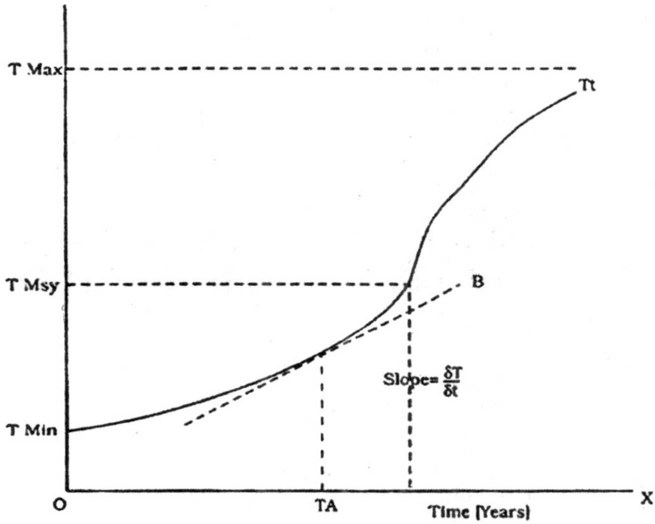

Logistic Growth Curve for a Biomass Stock

Figure 12

The growth curve Tt has a logistic shape. At any point on the curve, the growth rate is the slope of a line tangent to the curve. Thus at time TA, the growth rate corresponds to $\partial T/\partial t$ at point A. The maximum biomass, T max, will be determined by the carrying capacity of the environment. The maximum stock, Tmin, corresponds to a minimum self-sustaining population. If harvesting occurs below this point, the population will be too small to reproduce successfully.

4

EXTERNALITIES AND ENVIRONMENTAL IMPACT OF AQUACULTURE INDUSTRY

Aquaculture has been a remarkable economic growth sector in India during the past decades which has contributed significantly in earning foreign exchange as well as socio-economic benefits to the society. In the past, India was predominantly dependent on agriculture. For the export earnings and today the export of marine products has offered tremendous market potential to expand this industry in India.

Being more remunerative than agriculture and live stock husbandry, aquaculture is developing into a prime industry to tap the enormous turnover of bio energy to meet the challenges such as starvation and malnutrition posed by the burgeoning population. Aquaculture with shrimp farming in particular has become more popular in India as a solution to the problem of low income coastal farmers, leading to the rapid expansion of this industry in the rural areas. Aqua farming implies some form of intervention in the rearing process to enhance production through interaction with environment such as regular stocking, feeding, soil, water and stock management. The impetus given to the shrimp culture is mainly due to its lucrative foreign exchange earning capacity. However, these activities leads to adverse effects like outbreak of diseases and environmental hazards. Such exploitation of the environment invariably results in a set of intended and unintended results in varying degrees of severity causing environmental degradation which is further exasperated by the indiscriminate human interference.

It's quite obvious that aquaculture interacts with the environment and results overall in both positive and negative impacts on sustainable development. In a panoramic view, no doubt, shrimp farming is more prone to have high environmental costs, but can also be sustainable and profitable, if due care is given to a number of environmental management concerns for a balance between shrimp farming and environment. This dramatic expansion of the industry in India has caused serious concerns, especially in terms of environmental degradation and on socio-economic impacts along the coastal belts of Tamil Nadu and Andhra Pradesh. The areas under environmental threat lie along the coastal belts since most of the areas under aqua production lie in the marine and brackish water environments.

The land and water area are the two important pre-requisites for aquaculture development. The type of land used for shrimp farming has an effect on the success of the shrimp farming itself and the environmental impacts and conflicts with other people inhabiting the coastal areas. Shrimp farms have been constructed on a variety of coastal lands including salt pans, areas previously used for agriculture crops such as rice, sugar and ecologically important mangroves and marshes. Coastal shrimp culture also utilises considerable amount of fresh water for maintaining salinity in the ponds. However, the uncontrolled extraction of ground water has resulted in subsidence of coastal land and salt water intrusion in some areas causing major conflicts with agriculture and domestic uses. It is inferred in this context that a research on socio-economic and environmental impact of aquaculture in coastal areas of Tamilnadu and Andhra Pradesh is highly essential so that future possibilities of management of the aquaculture conflicts can be curtailed. It is also relevant to look into positive externalities when more noise is made about the negative side in order to arrive at sustainable aquaculture. The two major environmental concerns of prime importance in aquaculture are:

EFFLUENT DISCHARGES

The effluents from shrimp farms adopting intensive & semi intensive practice are not permitted since 1997. Intensive and semi-intensive culture practices involving high rates of stocking, feeding and water-flow contain solid and soluble wastes. Solid wastes consist mainiy of organic carbon and nitrogen compounds. The soluble wastes are derived from the decomposition and leaching of solid wastes. The Biochemical Oxygen Demand (BOD) of effluents is a valuable parameters for evaluating the palliative effects of wastes.

Discharge of the shrimp farm effluents can bring about one or a few of the following palliative effects on the receiving water.

(a) Hypernitrification and eutrophication
(b) Fall in DO
(c) Increase in sanitary indicator bacteria
(d) Increase algal blooms
(e) Increased 'sewage fungus'
(f) Increased macropytes
(g) Increased suspended solids
(h) Deposits of soils
(i) Discoloration of water
(j) Smell
(k) Bad taste of fish
(l) Changes in benthic fauna
(m) Deteriorated fishery
(n) Fish kills

IMPACTS OF AQUACULTURE IN TAMIL NADU AND ANDHRA PRADESH

India is primarily an agricultural country and most inland waters are utilized to a large extent in supporting agriculture. Similarly most aquaculture activities in India is primarily brackish water based and located at the tail end of the rivers are especially along the various deltas of the Ganges, the Godavari, the Krishna, the Cauveri etc. Among these deltas, over 75% of aquaculture development exists in the East coast, along the Bay of Bengal with high concentration in Andhra Pradesh and Tamilnadu. With the availability of extensive brackish water areas in these two states, coastal lagoons and low lying areas are being utilized for aquaculture purposes in the coastal districts of these two states. Therefore prime attention is focussed on the environmental impacts of aquaculture in these two states.

The major environmental impacts encountered in these coastal states due to aquaculture are :

- Impact on coastal land use
- Impact on soil texture
- Impact on the coastal ecosystem and its resources
- Exploitation of surface water and salination of ground water.
- Health hazards resulting in outbreak of diseases.
- Deterioration of water quality.

It has been reported that cases of over concentration and intensification of aquaculture industries in these two coastal states has severely enhanced the bio degradation of the water quality in the ambient areas.

Environmental Economists say reducing the pollution is one of the stepping stone for the development of the country as well as to mankind. Shrimp Cultivation at one side gives more income, employment and better standard of living at the same time on the other side is polluting soil and water. People who live nearby in Andhra Pradesh are affected by the Pollution a lot compared with Tamil Nadu. For example soil polluted in Andhra Pradesh is very high. Though much emphasis is given by the N.G.O's and the voluntary organisations against the impacts of aquaculture in these states, it is highly important to consider the high export oriented economic activity with much positive socio-economic implications in the upliftment of the coastal communities. Therefore, it is better to plan and regulate aquaculture in these states to maintain the sustained ecological balance and reap the positive socio-economic impacts.

ENVIRONMENTAL CONCERNS OF AQUACULTURE

Generally, shrimp culture impacts are focussed towards the potential environmental concerns. However, these in several instances, are construed to be real impacts, out of context and without facts and figures. Even when certain impacts are of local manifestation and of transient nature, these are extrapolated to space and time. The fact that many of the aquaculture practices are still based on empirical knowledge, market driven and profit motivated and result in situations of auto-pollution under certain farming practices causing more damage to culture production than to the general environment, confuses the perception of environmental damage. However, this is not to state that aquaculture cannot cause damage to the environment (Alagarswami, 1995). Over concentration and intensification can certainly result in degradation of water quality. Scientific data base need to be built up on a space and time scale to measure such impacts for making conclusions. The Government at the centre and states have come out with guidelines for promoting and regulating coastal aquaculture. The environmental aspects to be looked into sustainable development can be broadly categorised as:

PRE- DEVELOPMENT PHASE

- Public policy on aquaculture
- Land use policy and planning
- Laws of the land, as applicable
- Multi-user conflict issues
- Integrated coastal zone development, including coastal fisheries
- Exclusion of conserved areas (mangroves, biodiversity conserved zones)
- Site selection
- Water quality criteria
- Environmental carrying capacity
- Seepage abatement

- Negative feedback to aquaculture
- Environmental management plan

OPERATIONAL PHASE

- Quality control of stocking species
- Quality control of water
- Use of fertilizers, chemicals and drugs
- Quality and ration of feed
- Control of algal blooms
- Health management and disease control
- Waste treatment of the pond effluents and discharge
- Environmental monitoring

IMPACT ON LAND

Land being a prime component of aquaculture is found in the following proportions in Sirkali Taluk, a prime location of flourishing aquaculture in TamilNadu.

Sirkali taluk comprise of 583.73 Sq.km i.e. 58373 ha of land. The net sown agricultural area in the taluk accounts for about 57 per cent of the total geographical area. Agriculture has been the major occupation of the people in this area. About 1102 ha (less than 2 per cent) of land remains as forest land which is far below the national average of 23 per cent.

The area occupied by shrimp/prawn farms in the taluks of Sirkali, Tharangampadi and Nagapattinam is about 2000 ha, which is less than 2 per cent of the total geographical area. These farms have actually paved the way for the utilization of the barren, uncultivable lands. This area is situated at the tail end of the River Cauvery irrigationsystem and the prospects of cropping have been dim and disappointing due to inadequate and untimely water supply. Hence, the farmers were frantically looking for an alternative use of their lands or for disposing them off for good prices. The per capita available arable land in Sirkali taluk is 0.163 ha as compared to the national availability of arable land, 0.219 ha (*The Hindu*, 1999). As the size of the arable land is decreasing with the increasing population, it would be difficult to produce the staple food grains like rice and other cereals. But some of the agricultural farm owners have taken up shrimp farming for making quick and huge profits. Some others have sold their lands to private and Corporate bodies, interested in setting up aquafarms for earning huge profits in a short span of time.

The shrimp farming in Nagapattinam district commenced in a small-scale in 1991 and became intensive from 1993. Due to shrimp farming, the value of land has increased manifold. Before the commencement of shrimp farming, the land value was only about Rs. 18,000 to Rs. 20,000 per ha., but has increased to about Rs. 1.5 lakhs to Rs. 1.8 lakhs per ha., i.e. 10 times when shrimp farming gained popularity. The ownership pattern of land has also radically changed. About 20 per cent of the coastal land holdings were sold to big aqua farms as the size of the lands were small (less than one ha), (40 per cent due to high price, 30 per cent due to inadequately profitable crop production and 10 per cent because of non-availability of labour). Some entrepreneurs have not set up their farms after spending huge sums for buying the lands due to the present protests against the prawn farms. The price/value of land has come down now because of the prevailing situation in this area.

The traditional agriculturists in the coastal areas have profitably utilized the money realized from the sale of their lands to purchase interior fertile farm lands. Those who have purchased lands for shrimp farming are mostly from other regions and now they are in a fix and some of them have given their lands to the local farmers on lease for setting up shrimp farms.

IMPACT OF COASTAL AQUACULTURE ON ENVIRONMENT

The impetus given to shrimp aquaculture is mainly due to its lucrative foreign exchange earning capacity. In India this realization materialized only in last decade, which coincided with unprecedented pressure on natural resources such as water and land. From other countries of Asia, where coastal aquaculture took root sometime earlier, vast deterioration in water quality, habitat destruction and loss of bio-diversity are widely reported.

If not properly planned the spread of brackish water shrimp culture into other user area will lead to adverse effect on natural habitat and social customs. One perceptible change is that the coastal resources hitherto held as common property with easy and open access became unapproachable to the population that enjoyed the privilege for generations The local population that survived on such resources got uprooted.

AQUACULTURE VS WATER QUALITY

All the major shrimp farming countries of the world have faced environmental problems mainly due to unplanned and uncontrolled development propelled by greed and unlimited profit motives (Gomes, 1992). The rapid development of shrimp farms in South Asia has raised serious environmental concerns such as conversion of agricultural lands, salination of surface water resources, salination of soils in agricultural lands, pollution and disease problems. So the need to determine the environmental limits for sustainability of aquaculture is seriously reviewed by the people concerned with the industry.

Parthasarathy (1995) pointed out that many drinking water sources in villages adjacent to shrimp farms have turned saline due to the indiscriminate pumping of ground water by shrimp farms. The intrusion of seawater coupled with the seepage of effluents has caused the health hazards like Cholera, Malaria, Jaundice and Eye ailments. The Bhagavathi Environment Development Institute, Dindigul claims that an analysis of water samples from half a dozen villages in Sirkazhi taluk has shown a disturbing degradation in the quality of ground water. Hardness and alkalinity levels of water collected at 17 points in seven villages were alarmingly in excess of the prescribed tolerance limit of drinking water. These are attributed to shrimp farms setup along the coast in the past two years. But CMFRI (1995) reported that the quality of groundwater in the entire coastal area (Nagapattinam Qaid-e-Milleth district) is saline. As such implicating the very recently started shrimp farming for such development is not at all justified and that too in the absence of any data before shrimp farming came into operation for comparison.

ENVIRONMENTAL IMPACT OF SHRIMP FARM EFFLUENTS

The pollution caused by the water discharged from the shrimp farms is a matter of controversy. The fact is that the pollution from shrimp farm effluent is considerably less than that of domestic or industrial wastewater. However, effluent produced during pond cleaning has a much greater pollution potential. When significant concentrations of shrimp farm developed in areas with limited water supply, as for farms located in the Kandeleru creak area in Andhra Pradesh, a self pollution occurs, with shrimp farmers themselves being the most severely affected. The release of effluent, rich in organic matter, can be expected to result in siltation and changes in productivity and community structure of benthic organisms. The creaks and canals receiving the discharge also get silted up as a result of organic matter discharged from shrimp farms. There is a danger of depletion of dissolved oxygen levels in receiving waters. The discharge of nutrients carries the risk of eutrophication and algal bloom in coastal waters affecting the environmental conditions and ecology of the area. Again the environmental deterioration will work against the sustainability and play a major role in the development of disease problems with serious production losses. It is to be pointed out here that even though the disease outbreaks are directly linked to the environmental factors no conclusive study is available to understand the pathways of disease causing pathogens and the interaction involved.

A greater understanding of the relationship between shrimp stress, disease and pond production would certainly help to provide the basis for improved management of ponds. Managing the environment in a way, which ensures it, is suitable for the shrimp and not for the pathogen, is now recognized to be an important procedure put forward in disease control. This approach also put self-reliance and sustainability for development of farm level solutions. Due to the lack of awareness or neglect most of our shrimp farm projects are established without any environmental impact assessment that provides a means of examining sustainability during the planning of aquaculture projects. Therefore it is essential to give due consideration at the planning stage for:

(ii) the potential risks inherent in the site i.e., soil and water quality

(iii) the potential impacts on the external environment such as effects of effluent discharge potential impacts from the external environment namely, pollution from agricultural and industrial sources.

IMPACT ON COASTAL LAND USE

The development of shrimp culture has both positive and negative impacts on the coastal land use. A positive impact is that it increases the efficiency of the utilisation of the coastal area but at the same time it reduces the availability of other agricultural land. Further, the construction of shrimp ponds causes soil erosion and a reduction of the land productivity, environmental pollution and soil salinisation. It is noteworthy to mention that saline soil areas utilized for shrimp farming cannot be used for normal agricultural purposes after shrimp farming. However, this statement remains a controversial one since many aqua farms are being converted to agriculture fields in Andhra Pradesh.

INCREASED EFFICIENCY OF LAND UTILIZATION

At the outset of aquaculture practices, coastal lands previously barren were brought under culture, but however, in course of time even the fertile rice fields, conserved areas like the mangrove forests and salt farms were utilised for shrimp farming. This development in marine shrimp culture subsequently has reduced plantation and paddy field areas in the coastal areas. Increase in soil erosion, pond and dike construction also has caused accumulation of soil and sedimentation in the nearby area. At times during pond construction significant soil loss occurs and is washed down to the sea and nearby area. This is enhanced by the removal of pond sludge during pond preparation for each crop increasing soil erosion into the natural water resources or into the beach which is then washed down to the sea, eventually that may change the physical characteristics of the natural water resources on the sea bed in that particular area.

IMPACT ON SOIL

The Mangrove ecosystem is considered to be a dynamic environment which acts as a potential nursery ground for many aquatic organisms. However, with the advancement of aquaculture activities in these areas, rapid degradation of the environment and soil quality have taken place. Due to the impacts of shrimp farming, the organic content, phosphorus, potassium, magnesium, sodium and sulphate contents of the mangrove soil were found to be lowered and to the contrary increase in calcium, iron, aluminium and manganese contents were encountered to be high (Banchong, 1995). The pond and dike constructions in the mangrove areas for shrimp farms has eventually lowered the load of organic matter and exposes the pyrite in the lower level of soil to air. The oxidation of pyrite produces Fe_2 So_4 and H^+. These ions tend to increase the soil acidity which lowers the primary productivity of shrimp pond thereby reducing the growth rate of the aquatic organisms. The acidity of the soil is correlated with the quantity of iron, manganese and aluminium. The degradation of the soil was found due to intensive use of organic compounds and chemicals as medicines and fertilizers for shrimp farming. Therefore, proper aquaculture design and controlled application of the chemical compounds without intervening the sustainable ecosystem is warranted. Reports from N.G.O's have quoted that the country needs ecological aquaculture not intensive aquaculture where the yield is phenomenal but at the cost of long term ecological damage to the soil. (Swaminathan, 1995).

IMPACT ON THE COASTAL ECOSYSTEM

The aquaculture effluents discharged into the marine environment is yet another problem causing deleterious impacts on the survival of the coastal resources. The effects on the coastal habitats are mainly due to the improper saline water released as pond effluents which directly imposes a pronounced effect on both the marine and fresh water organisms. However, this appears to be incorrect since the effluents of the aquafarms consists of only biological wastes like feed remains made up of fishmeal and other fishery products and further the salinity remains constant since the water is pumped in from the natural source of the same salinity and this salinity is maintained for the successful growth of the culture.

IMPACT ON SURFACE WATER AND GROUND WATER

The salinisation of surface water is another water quality impact frcm shrimp farms to the receiving waters. It is reported that shrimp farm construction can potentially alter surface water flow patterns and water quality. Water flows were found to be affected by the temporary blockage of permanent division of canals and discharge of untreated pond effluents into the natural system was known to hinder the water quality. Further, due to seepage of saline water from the ponds into the ambient areas also leads to the salination of the ground water. There are cases of stratification occurring in the surface of fresh water zone with the mixing of deeper saline water that.will affect the agriculture land when the farmers unknowingly pump the salinised water into farm land which damages the land quality. The shrimp farmers directly discard waste water without treatment into the public canal or coastal area or river and inshore areas that causes general pollution and public health hazard problems.

Effective pumping of saline water in case of bore water dependent farms and fresh water in case of coastal farms result in fall of ground water table. The salinated ground water also affects the drinking water sources of the coastal villages.

Shrimp farming causes dispersion of salt into land around the shrimp farms there by increasing the salinity intrusion affecting the paddy fields and other plantations. The soil salinisation further resulted in devaluation of marginal agricultural land. Abstraction of fresh water from underground aquifers for intensive shrimp farming has also resulted in salt water intrusion and salinisation of fresh water aquifers. While fresh water aquaculture poses little negative impact on ground water and aquifers, brackish water aquaculture is detrimental to subterranean water resources. It is suggested that a system of geo-grid fabrics can be utilised in order to prevent salinisation of ground water (Isaac, 1995). This issue concerns the proper site selection and engineering rather than negative aspect of aquaculture.

OUT BREAK OF DISEASES

Disease outbreaks especially uncontrollable emergence of white spot (White spot syndrome virus) disease had given a death blow to the aquaculturists in Andhra Pradesh and Tamilnadu in 1994. Some shrimp farms suffered a serious setback during the year. As a result, shrimp production was very much affected and the shrimp farmers faced heavy losses. The environment responded with a negative feedback to shrimp culture due to a self pollution effect leading to disease outbreaks. This auto-pollution not only affected themselves but also affected wild stock. There is a definite possibility of infections being carried from one farm to the other through inflows from a common source. The disastrous collapse of the Taiwanese shrimp farming is partly attributed to the cause of contaminated drain water from adjacent ponds.

The quality of water in a shrimp culture pond includes less than 300 ppm of dissolved solids, pH range between 6.5 and 9.0, dissolved oxygen content greater than 3 ppm, calcium content less than 100 ppm and phosphorus and nitrate content less than 1 ppm. The release of inorganic nutrients from increased shrimp effluents due to intensive farming, cause 'eutrophication (increase in phytoplankton production) in the brackish water where the spent water is disposed. Shrimp effluents include chlorine (to purify water), antibiotics like chloramphenicol and malachite green which are used to control pest and diseases. Apart from this, the high protein diet of shrimps comprising chicken and pig excreta also pollutes the water. These wastes accumulating in the ponds by poor environmental conditions are the most important factors contributing to the outbreak of disease in the aquaculture system.

Shrimps stressed by poor pond bottom conditions may lead to viral diseases in shrimps like 'White spot disease' or 'Yellow head disease'(YHD). The bacterial diseases can be treated with antibiotics and before starting the treatment it is important to identify the cause of disease and determine the antibiotic sensitivity of the bacterial pathogens. Antibiotics may also accumulate in pond sediments and persist in the environment for a long time. Exposure to antibiotics would lead to the development of antibiotic resistance in the bacteria since bacteria are opportunistic pathogens. Such antibiotic resistant bacteria involved in shrimp infections at a later time may be difficult to treat due to the development of primitive immune system by which the resistance to disease gets increased by microbial cell components. Vaccines are known to induct resistance against disease (Karuna Sagar and Indrani Karuna Sagar, 1995).

Reports from the Chairman of MPEDA, K.B. Pillai have confirmed that the outbreak of diseases occurred as a result of contamination of seawater due to bacterial load in the post–monsoon season when the water flow to the sea is polluted by domestic waters and industrial effluents generated from aqua farms.

It is therefore important to mention that the effluents from aqua farms be treated before reaching the environment particularly when the organic load is high at time of harvest and also the use of secondary aquaculture can reduce the organic load in waste water. So such effluents need to be passed through primary sedimentation and secondary biological oxidation treatment before discharging into the water bodies.

SEDIMENT LOAD IN THE NATURAL ENVIRONMENT

The exponential growth of population, the rapid pace of industrialisation and urbanisation and increasing use of fertilizers and pesticides increase effluent loads directed into the coastal eco-system. Sediment material water borne suspended solids are dissolved nutrients can potentially create problems in the drainage canals and impact on the local aquatic and marine environment. The sediment loading in canals affects the source of water quality and availability to the near by shrimp farms which use the same supply system.

The effluent contains nutrient enriched waste waters that will affect the receiving environment. The post harvest flushing of pond bottom, can result in very high levels of nutrients and solids which will form into black mud. The receiving environment will undergo significant impacts from this material, unless the pond sediment is allowed to dry for a period and then removed from the ponds, without re-entry to the water discharge of the pond.

WATER QUALITY DETERIORATION

Waste water from shrimp farms is high in nitrogen, phosphorus, carbon compounds, organic matter, shrimp excretory products, plankton and some chemical and antibiotic residues. Most of the shrimp farms do not have water treatment systems and discharge the drain water directly to public water courses of sea. If the waste water is discarded without dilution or treatment, it will cause pollution to the environment. The discharge of pond effluent has led to water quality deterioration in irrigation canals and near shore coastal areas. The effluent water from shrimp ponds include, the water released during rearing to control the quality of water in the ponds, as well as the water discharged during harvesting of pond preparation for a new crop. This effluent comes from the high volumes of low concentration effluent and concentrated releases during harvest and the cleaning of shrimp ponds. The loading are substantially more in final stages of harvesting and cleaning of ponds when there is high concentration of both nutrients and organic matter.

It is suggested that the problem of environmental deterioration could be solved by using a closed water recycle of recirculation system so as to overcome adverse conditions like pollution that leads to outbreak of diseases.

IMPACT ON AIR

Generally there is no air pollution except the foul smell emanating sporadically near the aqua farm site. Some big farms have generator sets for meeting their electricity needs in times of power failure. These sets, when in operation, generate gaseous emissions which could be controlled by erecting suitable stacks of adequate height conforming to the Pollution Control Boards norms. Again, this sort of emission of gases like carbon monoxide takes place even in the agricultural activities, when the farmers use Kerosene/Diesel generator sets for pumping water to their lands. Air pollution dealing with the emission of obnoxious gases are components of chemicals but are generally common in agriculture and aquaculture

CHEMICAL IMPACT

Coastal aquaculture farms have not been scientifically designed and located, resulting in excessive ecological damage to the fragile coastal environment. The saline water intake and effluent discharge from aquaculture farms result in contamination of water, especially in the case of small shrimp farms which are closely huddled together and which have been set up with less capital investment but aiming at high profits.

EUTROPHICATION

When a stream or pond is heavily fertilised by degradable wastes, the stimulation of plant growth will 'age' it and eventually cause its death by choaking it with the plant growth. This process is called eutrophication. Indiscriminate release of enriched effluent water in water bodies creates eutrophication and enhancing of BOD subsequently affecting fauna causing either mortality or exodus. It is likely that the concentration of TSS, BOD, COD and nutrients in the farm effluent might increase towards the end of each crop. It is noticed that most of the larger farms are incorporating effluent treatment plant in their existing design. Effective use of effluent treatment system will reduce the concentration of these factors in the farm effluent. In the Uppanar estuarine system, a number of shrimp farms have been set up on both sides of the estuary.

They draw water in the salinity range of 6.1 to 35.6 ppt. They let out untreated effluent water back in the stream. However, the TSS, BOD, COD and nutrient levels have been within limits in many places with a few exceptions.

Marginally high BOD levels have been recorded in the outlet canals of some farms. The increase in the BOD was due to stagnation of water in the outer canal and not because of the farming activity. Marginal increase in the TSS was also noticed only in the outlets of small farms and this was due to high levels of TSS in the estuarine inlets themselves.

The concentration of heavy metals like iron was negligible in the effluents of all the farms. "Since the nutrients in the outlet was within permissible limits, it did not create plankton bloom in any of the areas except in the stagnant outlets of one non-functional farm". Further it has been reported that low level enrichment of seawater by farm effluents actually increases congregation of fish upto 10 times in the discharge areas fish and other marine life contribute to the eco-balance which in turn supports human life which is an important component of the biological sector.

BIOLOGICAL IMPACT

Since coastal aqauculture farms have not been scientifically designed and located they are resulting in excessive ecological damage. So small shrimp farms buy wild seed collected by the fishermen from creeks and sea. This indiscriminate, wild collection of seedlings from the coastal waters, creeks and estuaries results in reduction of their availability, in their natural habitations. This in turn affects the fishermen's catches of shrimps in natural surroundings and their income. (Juveniles) fish seeds bought from hatcheries have high mortality of 60%, where as natural fry collected from estuaries have better survival rate up to 90%. This leads to the threat of disappearance of mother shrimps and other wild creatures in the natural environment. However, it is also important to mention at this juncture that berried females (mother prawns) caught by the fishermen are sold by them to aquaculturalists for far higher prices like one berried female affording a price of Rs. 15,000-20,000. This cost price of one mother prawn far exceeds the whole day catch of fishes by a fishermen. This accounts to the better living of the fishermen in the coastal areas due to the advent of the aqua farms.

IMPACTS ON SHORE BIRDS

Several species of birds and mammals become closely associated with shrimp culture because of location of farms on or near their natural habitats. Many of them are predatory in habit and destroy substantial quantity of shrimp farm stocks. So the aquafarmer considers them a threat to his stock and takes all possible measures to prevent predation. From an environmental point of view, the farmers efforts to protect farm stocks by taking anti-predator measures can affect the population size or natural habitats of birds.

ENVIRONMENTAL EFFECTS OF EXOTIC SPECIES

The release of exotics into the environment can have adverse effects. Besides, predation or competition with local fauna, there are dangers of hybridization and reduction of genetic diversity. The inadvertent introduction of pathogens and diseases carried by the exotics is a serious danger. In view of above effects, exotic species of shrimps should not be encouraged for farming.

CONFLICTS OF AQUACULTURE

A number of shrimp farms have been set up violating many rules and there were no proper systems for supervising and monitoring these farms. This has resulted in conflicts in the use of common property resources. The shrimp farms fenced their area without giving any notice and did not allow the public, especially the fisherman community who were using the beaches for years together because of lack of proper rights to use common property resource. The shrimp farms have been set up without considering the hardships of the local fishermen community because of the open access to the seashore. Open access system has given rights to the fishermen for using the seafront for their livelihood. Likewise the owners of the shrimp farms just purchased the cultivable lands from the agriculturists and converted into aqua ponds. This is also resulting in conflicts with the users of land for agricultural activities. Some of the farms have not shown any concern when the ground water sources turned into brackish. Only a very few farms have made arrangements for the supply of sweet potable water to the local people. Such conflicts have made the local people to voice and protest severely against the shrimp farms.

CONFLICTS BETWEEN FISHERMEN AND AQUA FARM

The shrimp farms do not provide access to the beach for traditional fishermen who have to reach the sea from their villages. As aqua farms are located on the sea front and entry is restricted, the fisherman have to take a longer route to sea for their operations. The traditional, local fishermen, doing fishing for years are subjected to such hardships because of the newly emerging aqua farms.

SOCIAL CONFLICTS

Social conflicts arise between the nearly people and aqua farms due to salinisaion of drinking water, salinisation of land and fear of floods during the rainy season. It is reported that salinisation of land is spreading further and the wells yielded only salinised water. The agricultural farms adjoining the shrimp farms are reported to be affected. Aqua farms are constructed right on the banks of the creeks without leaving any space for draining of flood water.

SOCIO-CULTURAL IMPACTS

Shrimp culture is essentially a human activity which has varying socio-cultural and economic impacts on human communities involved. An appreciable number of rural people have found employment as owner operators or wage earners in shrimp farms, enhancing their economic standard. The state Government is leasing out sites to co-operatives or to poorer sections of society with a view to help the poor for earning cash benefits. Since market price of shrimp is very high, the overall socio cultural and economic standards of marginal and small-scale farmers will be certainly improved.

Shrimp farming suffers from lack of social acceptability. Indiscriminate conversion of agricultural lands into shrimp culture farms aggravated landlessness among farmers which has changed the land use patterns in the coastal areas.

The ownership pattern has radically changed due to various reasons. About 20% of the coastal land holdings were sold due to small size of the land (less than one ha) 40 per cent due to high price, 30 per cent due to inadequate profitable crop production and 10% because of non-availability of labour. The traditional agriculturist in the coastal areas have profitably utilized the money realized from the sale of their lands to purchase interior fertile farm for shrimp farming, are from mostly from other regions.

.Anti-aquaculture Sarvodaya leader Mr. Jagannathan's statement against unemployment in aquafarms is proved to be false since many employment opportunities are being offered to the local people and the agriculturists. Further, his statements that the land used for prawn farming could not be used for any purpose after a period of 10-12 years also proved to be wrong since many agriculture farmers are converting their paddy fields to aquaculture farms in TamilNadu. If this is the case in Tamilnadu, certain areas in Bheemavaram (AP) which were involved in aquaculture were converted again to agriculture fields to maintain rotation of crops and high yield both in aquaculture and agriculture and prevent outbreak of diseases.

It was also noted that only fallow lands and cultivable wastes area have been converted into prawn farms in Tamilnadu. It was noteworthy to mention that due to the persisting Cauvery water issue, farmers who were harvesting only one crop in Poompuhar area have given up agriculture and shrimp farm companies/ investors purchased fallow lands from them. In fact, it should be understood that that the shrimp companies came to the rescue of the worried farmers.

POSITIVE IMPACTS OF AQUACULTURE

Studying and understanding the environment in the context of aquaculture development are becoming imperative. The impact of aquaculture on environment is positive and bio-degradable wastes provide nutrition beneficial to aquaculture production otherwise it is mineralized by bacteria. Impacts of aquaculture on the environment include change to resources such as water and land and competition between users. Certainly aquaculture can contribute positively to environment in many ways a fact often not recognized in discussion of environmental forums.

HUMAN IMPACT

Human impact deals with the social, cultural and economic impact of aquaculture. Though aquaculture is also like agriculture and included in the primary sector, its social impact is significant. Local fishermen as well as agricultural farmers have found jobs in shrimp farms, though most of the owners of big farms have been from the urban areas. It has resulted in good relationship between the management and workers. The employees in the aquafarms are of the opinion that they get better wages in shrimp farms.

India has vast area suitable for aquaculture, which are presently unutilised and under utilised. At present only a fraction of this water spread is being used for aquaculture activities and thereby promoting economic welfare of the people by providing lucrative jobs in aquatic farms and also earning valuable foreign exchange.

Aquaculture is making it possible to rear various types of fish and shellfish, especially shrimps in India and thereby increasing the availability of food that too nutritive food to feed the ever increasing population of the country which has reached 1 billion mark recently, on 11th May, 2000. It is not wise to depend on agriculture especially wheat and paddy alone to meet the food requirements of growing huge population.

The depletion or standstill of capture fishery since 1970s and availability of vast stretches of brackishwater lands (1.2 mn sq.km) in India resulted in development of shrimp farming in India. Due to high profit and financial viability it has rapidly expanded. In Tamilnadu also, the aqua culture industry developed rapidly and is still being practised in spite of the

Supreme Court's order ban on aquaculture farms set up within 500 meters from the sea landward. Agriculture lands were purchased for the setting up of aqua farms. In Sirkali Taluk more lands have been purchased at high prices, but now most of them are remaining idle due to opposition from all walks of life.

ECONOMIC ASPECTS

As already mentioned, shrimp farms are highly profitable ventures, provided no viral diseases attack the animals. Shrimps, with unique taste, favoured all over the world as delicious dish, are cultured in many of the South East Asian countries, since the captured production remains at standstill. As there is suitable, ample space available in the country as well as in the State, shrimps culture is being encouraged. Shrimp farms have been set up in Tamilnadu only in meagre areas, when compared to Andhra pradesh, though the potentials are bright. Therefore , when analysing the economic status of the country, nearly 5000 crore rupees of revenue emerges from aquaculture production and export. Thus, it is important to consider the expansion of this industry on a still larger scale waiving the environmental aspects which is common on either side of the establishment of a flourishing industry.

IMPACTS OF AQUACULTURE IN TAIWAN, PHILIPPINES– A COMPARISON

There has been considerable expansion of aquaculture in the mangrove areas of some countries like Taiwan, Philippines and Indonesia. In Philippines, out of the total area of 500,000 ha, 322,154 ha, of mangrove area has been converted for utilization, of which 206,525 ha was under aquaculture. Taiwan had an area of 11,000 ha out of which 8000 ha under aquaculture. Production rates in shrimp culture have gone up to 20 tonnes per ha as in Taiwan and also in isolated cases in the Philippines, which practice intensive shrimp farming techniques. This is against an average of 500 kg per ha in the traditional exclusive culture practiced in the mangrove areas.

Taiwan, with only 8000 hectare land under culture had the highest production rates for shrimp industry over two decades and climaxed to a production of 89,622 tonnes in 1987. However, there was a sharp decrease to 43,887 tonnes in 1988 (Sheeks, 1989). The drop was almost entirely due to a sharp drop in the volume of shrimp production from 78,848 tonnes in 1987 to 30,603 tonnes in 1988. The crisis was caused by utter disregard for environmental health which led to serious diseases of epizootic proportions. Identifying the causes for the collapse it was found that viral (MBW), bacterial (Vilmi sp) and protozoon diseases were rampant.

Since the Taiwan experience of 1987, there has been an increasing realization towards sustainable development of aquaculture. Aquaculture sowing and diversification of species to make use of natural location advantages and environmental compatibility are being stressed.

Though many senses were considered as "waste land" most parts of the world and were either ignored or alased, until the 1960's (Snedakar, 1987), the ecological and economic values of mangroves began to be well documented. The role of mangrove forests in coastal protection (e.g., against storms and erosion), the perpetuation of coastal water quality and the maintenance and production of coastal fishery resources are worth mentioning. They also help the socio-economic development of the coastal communities by supplying seeds for aquaculture industries as well as providing the traditional sources of medicines, honey, firewood, fodder and timber. The two important mangrove ecosystem of Tamilnadu are:

1. Pichavaram Mangroves in Chidambaram.
2. Muthupet mangroves in Vedaranyam.

There are few economic activities which have globally withused high growth rates as the culture of shrimp in coastal areas of a large number of countries, situated both in the eastern and western hemisphere during the past decade. The rapid development has been accompanied by many controversies resulting in a closer look at the environmental and socio-economic impacts of shrimp aquaculture. Its unregulated growth, especially in the east coast states of AP and TN has been a matter of serious concern and has been resulted in a landmark judgement by the supreme court of India on a public interest litigation in 1994 field by Shri.S.Jagannathan, Chairman, Tamilnadu Gram Swaraj Movement.

The Hon'ble court by its order of December 12, 1996, directed all the respondent states not to permit the setting up of any industry or the construction of any type on the area atleast upto 500 mts from the seawater at the maximum high tide. Apart from this, a special team from NEERI, Nagpur was appointed to investigate the impacts on the environment due to aquaculture. Following reports submitted by the NEERI experts, the Hon'ble court issued interim orders banning conversion of agricultural lands and self farms into commercial aquaculture, with drawl of ground water for aquaculture purposes and setting up of shrimp farms or any aquaculture farms in the area of dispute in the future.

In India, though many species of shrimps/prawns are available, with a wide distribution, *Penaeus monodon* commonly called 'Giant Tiger shrimp' and *P. indicus* commonly called 'white shrimp' form the main products of the aquaculture industry in India. Among these, Tiger shrimp is being considered for culture by a majority of the shrimp farmers in Tamilnadu mainly due to its age size and fast growth rate in the farming systems. They are generally collected in land based ponds or impoundments. To this clean water in utilized from the natural sources (creeks/canals/seekhi) for the optimum and hygienic growth and better survival during the crop tenure. The prime objective of the culture is to provide a good quality environment in ponds to present stress, immunize the risk of diseases, and to enhance survival rate and production.

In average rate of 500 kg – 1500 kg (0.5 – 1.5 ton) is expected per crop/hectare by adopted a semi intensive culture system (scientific farming practice in low input systems). In traditional shrimp farming systems, the majority of young shrimps are trapped in brackish water impoundments and allowed to grow with the introduction of scientific shrimp farming with selected stocking, the requirements for seed has increased and the controlled production of shrimp seed in sea water based net drain is practiced in the states of Tamilnadu and Andhra Pradesh.

Aquaculture has developed rapidly over the last there decades to become an economic activity worldwide. It has confronted many of the developmental problems in this relatively short period including sector competition, over production, trade restrictions, over capitalization and concerns over environmental inputs. Aquaculture, as with all agricultural enterprises, is dependent on natural resources. The optimum and sustainable use of natural resources for aquaculture (and agriculture) can lead to profitable economic gains, although if badly planned and managed, it can also lead to short and long term economic loss (Philips, 1995). (Philips, M.J. 1995. Aquaculture and the Environment–striking a balance. Proc. INFOFISH–AQUATECH '94–Conference on aquaculture towards the 21st century, Colombo, Srilanka, 29-31, Aug. 1994).

Aquaculture can be considered as an integral part of the natural environment, and the interactions between aquaculture and the environment are inevitable.

The major national resources required for aquaculture are land, water and biological inputs such as seed and feed. The manner in which the natural resources and used for aquaculture are the key to its economic success and sustainability.

In considering the interaction between aquaculture and the environment, it is essential to consider the environmental impacts related to aquaculture. These include the probable impacts of aquaculture operations on water land and other resources required by other aquaculturists or other user groups. It is important to recognize that the impact(s) may be negative or positive. "It may be also mentioned here that aquaculture can certainly contribute positively to environmental improvement in many ways, a fact often not recognized in many discussions on environmental impacts of aquaculture (Philips, 1995).

IMPACT OF AQUACULTURE WITH SPECIAL REFERENCE TO SIRKALI TALUK, TAMIL NADU

Most environmental problems stem from a combination of two broad set of factors: pressure factors such as population growth, human and economic activity and poverty on one hand, and enabling factors, such as market, government and institutional factors which allow the "pressure" to cause environmental damage (Markandya, *et al*, 2000).

The environment that contributes to the well being of the flora and fauna, need to the sustained by way of food chain. Aquaculture is an important link of the food chain encompassing the entire hydrosphere. Aquaculture refers to the practices involved in the farming of economically important aquatic animals and plants under controlled conditions. It includes the culture of fish, prawn, oyster, mussels, clams, etc., Shrimps of various species are cultured in brackish water farms extensively. They constitute one of the most important fisheries in India, especially from the point of view of their export values. Common varieties that are suitable for Indian conditions are *P. Monodon, P. Indicus and Meta penaeus dobsonii.*

Different types of localized methods of shrimp culture have been followed in India. The modern method includes larva collection and hatchery methods. Under hatchery method, separate hatcheries are functioning for the purpose of producing larva through modern scientific methods and these post larva of particular size are purchased and grown into adults with additional feeding in brackish water ponds. The production levels range from 200–300 kilos per hectare per crop to 10–20 tons that is 10,000–20,000 kilos per hectare per crop, depending upon the type of cultivation.

5

MANAGEMENT GUIDELINES FOR SUSTAINABLE AQUACULTURE

Intensive shrimp culture systems are rated as less favourable than extensive or semi intensive due to their impact on the environment. Before the construction of the farm, it is necessary basic data to have through well planned environmental assessment studies. Regular monitoring should be carried out after farming has started to determine the appropriateness and efficiency of the method adopted. Environmental Impact Assessment (EIA) which involves the analyses of the various aspects of the project with environmental quality. Since the rearing of aquatic animals requires additional labour, skill and special installations, the economic viability of aquaculture depends on a large number of interacting factors, which are more often sociological than technological and vary from region to region. The degree of success achieved also varies from one location to the other with respect to particular species used for cultivation. Successful aquaculture requires a complete management over the entire lifecycle of the organisms used as 'crop'. Control over reproductive biology, knowledge of food habits and mode of nutrition, types of diseases, availability of economically sound techniques of aquaculture engineering, etc are some of the factors which would determine the cost benefit ratio. In the near future it is hoped aquaculture as an industry would enjoy the same success as poultry framing has achieved in India. About three decades ago investment in poultry framing was considered risky, because of several bacterial and viral diseases as epidemics wiping out the entire poultry farm within a short time.

The greatest set–back in aquaculture industry has occurred because of unproven propaganda that aquaculture practices harm or degrade the adjoining agricultural land, pollute the nearby wells used for drinking water by turning them brackish. Thus, it is alleged that the environmental considerations are being sacrificed because of profitability.

The problem seems to be of socio–economic-cum political nature. However, this should not restrict the spread of aquaculture farms, which are urgently needed to produce quality protein food for domestic and foreign markets. The total shrimp production from aquaculture in India is 80,000 tonnes. This is rather modest when compared to a small country like Thailand where shrimp production through aquaculture, is of the order of 3,00,000 tonnes.

Aquaculture is somewhat similar to agriculture in the sense that it cannot be carried out economically just any where. A site for aquaculture, therefore must have certain prerequisites. Like sufficient depth of water, suitable temperature, practically throughout the year, optimum salinity and fertility of water. In agriculture only the top most soil, some 15 cm thick, sustains most of the food production. In aquaculture it is not only the top most layer but the entire water column, from surface to several meters depth is available for cultivation (Qasim, 1997).

Shrimp culture and environmental preservation must be achieved as a unified motto for sustainable development. (Supreme Court directives dicatate this).

1. It is suggested that no commercial coastal aquaculture activity should be undertaken even beyond the 500 metre High Tide Line (HTL) unless a comprehensive and scientific Environmental Impact Assessment (EIA) study is undertaken.
2. The environmental management plan (EMP) should be approved by the respective Pollution Control Board

of the concerned state and the Ministry of Environment and Forests.

3. The existing criteria for site selection should be reviewed and consideration should be given to long term capacity of the area to sustain aquaculture development.
4. The use of ground water for aquaculture should be banned and the rights of the coastal communities should be protected.
5. A minimum distance of 50-100 mts should be maintained between the aquaculture site and the near by agricultural land.
6. Aquaculture farms should be located at least 100 mts away from a smaller village and 300 mts away from a village of higher population.

These guidelines will ensure sustainable development and management of brackish water aquaculture.

NEED FOR NATURAL RESOURCE MANAGEMENT

Any development may have some ill effects also, that too in the initial stages. After understanding the nature of the problem, it is possible to solve it. This is the case of the shrimp industry also. Development activities, in general, are associated with some degree of depletion of resources. When the supply of resources is plenty in relation to its demand problems are not acute. With the increase in population, the awareness of the people to live better lives and with the technological revolution, resources are fast depleting. Some of these resources are non-renewable and so they may not be available for the generations yet to come. The renewable resources also need careful management, since they are not sufficient in relation to demand for it. Ground water is renewable if properly managed. On the other hand, groundwater is drawn for use at present, without knowing whether it gets recharged or not. It takes many years for rain water or stream water to enter into the deep layers of earth and stay there.

Proper land lease policy will be very helpful in making the landless labourers become aqua farmers, which in turn will help the aqua farmer. Setting up of aquafarms based on co-operative principles will be helpful to the small farmers, as well as, to the industry. It will improve socio-economic conditions of the people in the region.

If shrimp industry is to thrive, the conflicts between aquaculture and agriculture and also the conflicts between aquaculture and other uses of coastal area should be minimised. If the fishermen and landless agricultural labourers are encouraged to practice shrimp culture, unwanted clashes and conflicts would be avoided without any loss of foreign exchange. Though shrimp aquaculture is polluting the surroundings, if proper measures are introduced the level of pollution will become tolerable and the loss or damage will become manageable. This is not the only industry which is polluting the water or land. Industries like dyeing, leather processing also do the same. When these industries. are allowed to function with necessary checks, the aquaculture industry may also be permitted with certain provision to minimize the pollution problem.

Efforts should be made to ensure that the local people are motivated to accept the steps taken to protect the environment. Without the co-operation of the local people, any solution will not be a lasting one. The 'precautionary' principle as well as 'Pollutor pays' principle should be used wherever necessary. This suggestion has originated from the verdict of Supreme Court of India. EIA, (Environment Impact Assessment) must be made compulsory wherever necessary notably in aquaculture.

Considering the benefits received, disadvantages experienced and the favour shown by the general public as a group for the analysis, the results show an independent behaviour. Whereas, any one among the above group is considered individually, the results of the analysis show a dependent nature. Hence, the above results of this analysis from primary data leads to an elaborate analysis of each individual variable. The possibilities of analysis along these lines may be explored in future.

Various government authorities and research institutes, as also private sector and coastal management projects could organise and exchange information periodically and regularly. A specific system may be evolved to help improve cross - sectoral co-ordination and co-operation in the development and management of coastal areas.

The marine products exports from India depend heavily on the availability of shrimp as this single item commands very high unit value combined with heavy world demand. In India we are facing a near stagnation or decline in the marine fisheries production; especially with respect to shrimp. The limited nature of the resources is being realized of late and the accusing finger is pointing to the indiscriminate exploitation, with considerable investment, beyond sustainable limits. The efforts are now on for production through aquaculture. The initial success beyond expectations has attracted huge investment in this sector and the tempo is on.

NEED FOR WATER MANAGEMENT

The discharge of dissolved organic matter from metabolites and decomposition of uneaten food and shrimp faeces in to the sea from intensive shrimp farming operations has been stated to cause considerable harm resulting in fish death and foul smelling of water in many wetland areas. Therefore, it is inferred that water treatment facilities are compulsory for farms.

Water management and water quality control in aqua farms can be subdivided into three phases viz. (i) Inlet water management (ii) Daily water management (iii) Control discharge water management. Frequent exchange of water facilitates the maintenance of the water quality. It also prevents the accumulation of waste products, trace metals, depletion of organic compounds and accumulation of waste products that results in an increased Biological Oxygen Demand (BOD) and Chemical Oxygen demand (COD) levels in the pond.

Thus, the characteristics of the discharged water is a direct reflection of the internal process involved in water quality management at all the three stages viz. inlet water, daily pond water and discharge water. It is therefore sought to be highly essential for maximising the shrimp production. The aqua farm discharge does need to be regulated, both to protect the industry and the environment. Further, regulations governing aqua farms discharge need to be developed.

CONTROL OF DISEASES

It may be recalled that shrimp farms in coastal Andhra Pradesh faced a massive viral attack resulting in large-scale mortality in the ponds. The MPEDA has undertaken a study to ascertain the causes of the disease with remedial measures and recommended a break in culture operation of at least one crop. It declared a crop holiday for at least four - five months and appealed to all farmers to keep the pond empty and dry and to introduce effluent treatment of ponds, to avoid reoccurrence of the disease in future. Opinions differed widely as to what caused the out break of diseases in Andhra Pradesh and Tamil Nadu.

Some experts say that the diseases are due to the viral infections of Hypodermal and Hematopoietic Necrosis (HHNA). This virus appears to be highly virulent causing 80 - 90% cumulative mortality within two weeks, particularly in post larval and juvenile stages. Others name it as (SEMBV) Systematic Ectodermal and Mesodermal Baculo Virus. This virus is suspected to be the major cause of mass mortalities of cultured shrimp in India during 1994-95 when the affected shrimps were found to develop white spots on their body. Further, some term it as monodon baculovirus (MBV) as the causative organism for the disease.

There are also opinions that the whole situation might have been due to the cyclone with heavy rains and consequent changes in environmental conditions such as sudden reduction in atmospheric and water temperature, lowering of water salinity from over 25 ppt to less than 5 ppt, inflow of large volume of water from the land and paddy fields which contained insecticides and pesticides in heavy concentration into main water bodies like creeks and sea and from which shrimp ponds pumped water for exchange without assessing the quality of water. All these factors were presumed to have caused severe stress for the shrimps making them less immune to the attack of pathogens. Therefore, farmers should take necessary precautions to prevent further attack by the pathogens.

1. After ensuring the ponds have dried up sufficiently (cracks to be developed at least 4-6 cm deep) plough and replough the ponds 2 to 3 times.
2. Leave it exposed to sun for ten days.
3. Apply lime at 2 tonnes/ha for disinfecting the soil and then fill the ponds as per the usual procedures for pond preparation.

As the first step, MPEDA have suggested a crop holiday. To ensure the restart of the system in a prudent manner, the following steps are suggested to ensure that the disease infection does not arise again.

SUSTAINABILITY IN SHRIMP AQUACULTURE

In spite of having abundant brackish water swamp and coastal saline tracts, where nothing of commercial importance can be grown, considerable encroachment is taking place in productive agriculture land for conversion of aquaculture farms. In an unconfirmed report nearly one lakh ha. of land under food crops has been lost to aquaculture during the past four to five years in Andhra Pradesh. This conversion of agriculture land into aquaculture destabilizes the social system in many ways. It may be immediate economic benefit to some people. The small holders of such land may sell out their tilling plot at a premium price and get rich over night. But in that process he is loosing the field that sustained the life for generations.

OVER EXPLOITATION OF RESOURCES

The land and water are the pre-requisite for aquaculture development. The type of land used for shrimp farming has an effect on the success of shrimp farming itself environmental impacts and conflicts with other people inhabiting or using coastal areas. Shrimp farms have been constructed on a variety of coastal lands including saltpans; areas previously used for agriculture crops, such as rice, sugar and coconut, abandoned and marginal land, and wet land, including ecologically important mangroves and marshes.

In the traditional shrimp/fish filtration system that still exists in the states of Kerala and West Bengal the preference is for low-lying (intertidal) coastal wetlands. The demands of tide-fed coastal farms were the order of the day when shrimp culture remained with low cost technology. The introduction of scientific management system with high inputs, aiming at higher unit production, resulted in the search for supra-tidal land, above the maximum tide level, where ponds are comparatively easy to construct, drainable and soils are normally more suitable. By bringing in saline water, where previously there was no tidal effect, will result in salination of soil surrounding shrimp farms that may result in devaluation of often already marginal agriculture land and adverse effects on existing agricultural farms.

The other encroachments for shrimp farms are taking place in mangroves. In Thailand, Taiwan, Philippines, etc. the expansion of shrimp culture has led to destruction of mangroves. The loss of mangrove area can lead to ecological, economic and social impacts. Biologically, mangroves are important breeding ground or nursery area for many commercially important finfish, crustacean and mollusks. It has been reported from Thailand and Bangladesh that the expansion of shrimp farming into mangrove areas has lead to reduction in fish catches and declining socio-economic conditions for traditional coastal fishermen.

The mangrove also contributes to the sustainability of other human activities through coastal water quality regulation and shoreline protection. It is alleged that the carry over effect of the destruction of mangroves for short-term benefits will lead to greater economic effects in the long run. When we think of sustainable shrimp aquaculture it is necessary to keep the mangroves free from encroachments. It is also recognized that shrimp farms on mangrove land often support profitable shrimp culture for only short period. In other words mangroves are not normally the places for sustainable shrimp farming. The acid sulphate soils common in mangroves also can affect the sustainability of shrimp faces very badly.

The positive effects of retaining mangroves for the sustainability of shrimp farms also have to be considered. The coastal ponds if constructed behind the mangrove buffer zones get the protection from several physical hazards and also may favourably influence water quality in the farming areas. Mangroves have potential to remove excess nutrients, reduce suspended solids, remove heavy metals and absorb toxic hydrocarbons. Considering all these aspects a mangrove coastal buffer zone is essential to sustainable shrimp culture. To enable the development of sustainable shrimp farming it is necessary to prepare an area-wise master plan demarcating the area considered suitable, the areas that have to be retrained untampered with existing type of utilization and a buffer zone between shrimp farms and agricultural land and/or mangroves.

SUSTAINABILITY AND WATER SOURCE

Water with required quality and quantity will be required for different stages of shrimp farming. In the shrimp hatchery unpolluted seawater is required for brood stock maintenance, spawning, larval rearing and culture of food organism. Potable water is required in sufficient quantities for drinking and cooking food for the workers. The grow out farm ponds need sea/brackish water, free from agriculture, domestic and industrial pollution and also within the required salinities, pH and temperature ranges. The use of microbial contaminated water resulting in a grinding halt of shrimp farming in Andhra Pradesh is fresh in our memory. The quality of water and even the impacts from external environmental changes pose threat to the sustainability of shrimp culture. The higher water demand of more intensive culture is such that demand can easily outstrip supply in areas with poor tidal flushing.

CARRYING CAPACITY OF AQUACULTURE ENVIRONMENT

In coastal areas, the integration of aquaculture into integrated coastal area management should be strongly encouraged as a means of ensuring equitable use of resources. Every culture system and environment has a limited capacity to accept environmental impacts, e.g., to absorb pollutants without harmful environmental change. The capacity of a unit area to sustain biological production is often referred as "Carrying Capacity". The carrying capacity of an area can substantially be augmented through management measures. However, it is to be within an extended limit and not beyond that. The carrying capacity and its limits can be assessed by proper methods developed in recent years.

Presently shrimp industry is facing lot of problem in India. Generally people are of the opinion that the deterioration of drinking water quality is due to aquaculture. This presentation clearly brings out the fact that drinking water quality is not affected by shrimp culture in coastal habitats.

SOURCES OF WATER POLLUTION

Pollutants discharged into the water cycle are derived from there main sources: human and live stock waste (mainly bio-degradable organic products), discarded industrial products and industrial wastes (often toxic and accumulating readily in food chain), and agricultural chemicals (fertilizers and pesticides). Apart from the direct sources of pollution there are other means, which lead to the contamination/unsustainability of ground water. There is over exploitation of ground water for agricultural purposes, land resources and surface water resources. Large-scale land subsidences have taken place in Philippines (Primvera, 1994) and Taiwan (Chen, 1990). In India the problem of arsenic pollution has been experienced in West Bengal, where, the ground water in seven districts, covering 560 villages is affected by arsenic. More than 200,000 people are suffering from arsenic related problems (Mandal et al., 1996). The heavy withdrawal of ground water and the underground geochemical reaction underground may be the reason.

DEGRADATION OF MANGROVES FOR AQUACULTURE

Mangroves are endangered by hostile helerates and human abuse in the past (Kathiresan, 1995 a). This has resulted in the fast destruction and degradation of the mangroves that have already caused coastal erosion and decline in fishery potential in Tamilnadu. The coastal belt of Vedaranyam in Tamilnadu has lost nearly 40% of its mangrove area utilized for various purposes, which has led to the reduction of 18% of fishery resources with 13-year period from 1976-1989 (Padmavathi, 1991). Mangroves have been exploited by various farms of pressures viz. agriculture, industries, fuel wood extraction and diversion of water for irrigation and aquaculture (shrimp culture), which was carried out at the expense of mangroves in the early 1990's (Franklin and Palanivelu, 1989).

Though degradation of mangroves for aquaculture activities have taken place significantly in other states of India like Andhra Pradesh, the mangroves of Tamilnadu that exists in Pichavaram and Muthupet are well conserved without any interference of the aquaculture activities. The only problem encountered in these mangroves regions is cattle grazing, indiscriminate woodcutting for fuel in Pichavaram and Muthupet. Other factors involving constructions of urban development and industrialization also account for the degradation of mangroves. The survey hitherto undertaken in these areas has emerald no aquaculture activity being carried out in the vicinity of mangroves of Tamilnadu. It is understand that after the verdict of the Supreme Court on 11 December 1996 to the Aquaculture Authority of India, proper measures are enforced to curb any such activities to preserve the posture beauty of these natural resources, which act as the major nursery grounds for the shrimps.

Brackish water aquaculture in the mangrove rich areas of the coastal zones has been practiced traditionally. Thus sites were considered suitable for farming due to the tidal flow, fresh water influx and availability of seed resources. The last two decades have seen a great expansion of this activity, with commercial shrimp culture as the most dominant component planned conversion of mangrove forest areas to aquaculture focus is the outcome of these efforts.

SHRIMP AQUACULTURE IN THE INTERNATIONAL ARENA

Today there are 106 countries engaged in shrimp farming and 16 countries alone account for 85 to 90 per cent of shrimp supply in the world. Shrimp accounts for 20 per cent of world seafood production and 30 per cent of total world trade in seafood. The cultured world shrimp production has increased from 84,000 tons in 1982 to 1,15,320MT tons in 2003. The percentage share of cultured has increased from 4.8 in 1982 to 25 in 1989 and this started declining from the year 1990 due to viral attack in the shrimp farms in the South East Asian countries. Again the percentage share has increased to 29.7 in 1994. Thailand, Indonesia, Taiwan, Philippines, Ecuador and Vietnam are among the top world shrimp producing countries.

SHRIMP FARMING IN INDIA

The commercial-scale shrimp farming using semi-intensive method started only in late 1980s and early 1990s with the setting up several large ventures in the coastal regions of Andhra Pradesh and Tamil Nadu. The export of the marine products from India was gradually increased from 15,732 tonnes in 1961-62 to 4,67,297 tonnes in 2002-03 and it has increased to 612641 tonnes in 2006-07. Shrimps are most important item contributing about 67% of the total value of export. India, though a minor player in the total seafood trade, enjoys a fairly prominent position in the world production of shrimps and commands an 8 per cent share in the world trade in shrimp in terms of exports.

India is endowed with rich natural resources in the form of brackish water and estuaries for taking up shrimp culture in the coastal zone of the country. The estimated potential brackish water area available in India is about 1.4 million i.e., 14 lakh hectares, of which only an area of around 82,540 hectares is utilized for shrimp farming , mostly adopting traditional practices in spite of "extreme focus" status given in our national plans in the late 80s and 90s to increase exportable production.

Shrimps are commonly known as prawns and are held to be the "Gold of the Sea" in the popular eye. The inadequacy of the catch in natural waters and high price in the international market impelled many countries to achieve higher levels of production through aquaculture using modern techniques. The major irritants to the progress of aquaculture are held to be water pollution due to salinisation and the very many conflicts that arise due to common property resources and rights. The promotion of aquaculture is considered a must in many developing countries to combated malnutrition and under nutrition. Apart from its nutritional advantages, aquaculture is a major employment provider and income generator, especially in the economically depressed and socially deprived rural areas. There are many ways in which aquaculture aids social upliftment helping to maximize the use of idle or marshy lands. It is also an excellent source of foreign exchange earner. The establishment of and growth of related industries, such as manufactured of formulated feed milling, ice manufacture, net manufacture and cold storage are added advantages to economic growth.

SHRIMP FARMS IN TAMILNADU

There are nearly 250 aquaculture farms in the state covering water spread area about 4450 hectares. Nearly 50% of the aquaculture farms (648) in the state, covering a water-spread area of about 1480 hectares are located in Nagapattinam district. More than half the numbers of farms are creek based and only 229 farms within the CRZ are sea based.

IMPACTS: SHRIMP AQUACULTURE

In any environment there are bound to be both positive and negative impacts. The areas covered for analysis will include nature (which comprises the aspects such as physical, chemical and biological), human (which includes economic, social and cultural aspects) and national (which studies the areas like GDP, foreign exchange and food security). The area occupied by shrimp farms in the taluks of Sirkali, Tharangampadi and Nagapattinam is about 2000 hectares, which is less than 2% of the total geographical area. These farms have actually paved way for the utilization of barren and uncultivable lands. But some of the agricultural landowners have converted their lands into aquaculture farms and some others have sold their lands to private and corporate bodies interested in setting up aqua farms.

Shrimp culture has helped the area directly and indirectly with more business and economic activities in the region. The percentage share of shrimps in the total exports of marine products from India has declined from 117508 tonnes in 2000-01 to 135949 tonnes in 2007-08 (MPEDA-2008). Shrimps are the most important item contributing about 65% of the total vale of export of marine products. The share of Tamilnadu in the total exports of shrimps from the country ranges between 25% to 30% in terms of quantity and 30 to 35% in terms of value. [MPEDA-(2002-2003].

Fisheries occupy a prominent place in the economy of the country as well as the state by way of providing cheap nutritive food and employment opportunities. Aquaculture is widely accepted as the only major industry for maintaining even the present levels of global consumption of aquatic proteins.

Well planned environmental assessment studies even before the construction of farms, proper sanction and regular monitoring will be needed to safeguard and maintain the fragile coastal environment. With the introduction of various measures like the CRZ and Aquaculture Authority it is hoped that aquaculture as an industry would enjoy the same success as poultry farming has achieved in India.

SOILS OF TAMILNADU

Tamilnadu state lies between 76°14′-80°21′E longitude and 8°4′-13°54′ N latitude. It is bounded on the east by the Bay of Bengal on the south by the Indian Ocean on the north by Karnataka and AndhraPradesh and by Western Ghats and Kerala on the west. The total geographical area of the State is about 13.0 m ha. Geological formations: Rocks of Archaean age are extensively exposed and sediments ranging from Gondwanas to recent age are confined mostly to the eastern coast region. The crystalline rocks exposed include the rocks of charnockite group, Khondalite group and schists, traversed dy ultramafic, basic granite and syenite instrusives. Upper Gondana rocks, mostly comparing pink and white shales and feldspathic sand stones, are considered to be of mid-Triassic to lower Cretaceous in age. The sediments consisting mostly of clays, sands, limestone extend in age from the Anomanian to Danian. They are succeeded by sand stones and clays, considered to be of mid-Pliocene age. Formation of Pleistocene and recent age includes alluvium in deltaic regions and river valleys and coralline lime-stone in parts of Gulf of Mannar.

Physiography: Tamilnadu can be divided into 4 physiographic regions, viz., coastal plains, eastern ghats, central plateau and western ghats.

Coastal plains: The coastal plains stretch from Pulicat lake in the north to Cape comorin (Kanyakumari) in the south. This has three sub-regions, viz., (1) the northern plain consisting of Chengalpattu, a major part of South Arcot, eastern part of North Arcot and northern parts of Tiruchirapalli districts, (2) the Cauvery delta consisting of Thanjavur and part of Tiruchirapalli districts and (3) southern coastal plains shared by Ramanathapuram, Tirunelveli and Kanyakumari districts.

WATER QUALITY PROBLEMS AND POLLUTION

Water is one of the essential commodities which any human and other living population require for the in survival. Top priority is given by all sectors for estimating/quantifying and augmenting of resources of a region. However, experience shows that equal importance is not being given to the quality aspects of water, especially of pollution and contamination.

While surface water, which is mainly derived from rainfall, is generally free from harmful constituents; the groundwater, which is hidden in the subsurface soil strata, is subject to change in quality and its composition by way of adding salts from the soil strata. In coastal areas, the groundwater being in contact with seawater is always under stress and strain and its quality varies depending on the equilibrium conditions maintained between fresh and saltwater which in turn is controlled by the quality of groundwater extracted in the area.

The quality issues of groundwater are fourfold:

1. Groundwater being brackish water or saline depending on the geological strata, rock types, etc.
2. Pollution due to industrial and municipal discharges.

3. Contamination of groundwater aquifers in coastal region, mostly by seawater, backwaters, estuaries, etc.,
4. Contamination of groundwater due to the application of agro-chemicals and pesticides for agricultural purposes.

The groundwater wing of P.W.D. has taken up a detailed study of groundwater quality in the state of Tamil Nadu. In order to heave control over water quality in the State, the department is monitoring water levels and water quality in about 2100 shallow observation wells. Water samples from these wells are collected and analyzed for their chemical constituents twice every year.

GROUNDWATER POLLUTION DUE TO SEAWATER INTRUSION

Another type of pollution is from seawater intrusion into the inland aquifers. The range of intrusion studied by this department varies from 2 km to 8 km. The area mainly affected are being Kuttam area in Tirunelveli, Kattabomman district, Athidsuyapuram, Puthantharuvai in V.O. Chidambaranar district, east of Tiruvarur in Nagapattinam Quaied-E-Milleth district and Minjur area in Chengalpattu MGR district. The long-term data of Minjur area shows that seawater intrusion is advancing inland with time. The electrical conductivity ranges from 3000 to 10,000 micro sidemen's/cm in these areas, and this effect us noted down to 40-50 mts. This phenomenon of seawater intrusion is due to large-scale groundwater extraction.

UNREGULATED GROWTH

The development of modern shrimp aquaculture farms started in a small way in the mid-eighties when some entrepreneurs and technocrats obtained the technology from the demonstration projects of scientific research and promotional institutions and successfully engaged in profitable shrimp culture. Government organizations like the Marine Products Export Development Authority (MPEDA), which is under the Ministry of Commerce, played a major role in promoting shrimp aquaculture in view of the foreign exchange it could bring to the country. Banks and financial institutions came forward to support the new industry, which appeared to be attractive.

The post 1991 liberalization era saw many corporate sector giants investing in shrimp aquaculture and setting up 100 per cent export oriented units (EOUs), raising finances in the stock market. The phenomenal profits in the business also attracted small entrepreneurs, farmers and even some fishermen to shrimp aquaculture. In Andhra Pradesh, the area under shrimp aquaculture grew exponentially from around 8,000 hectares in 1991-92 to about 53,000 hectares in 1994-95.

The rapid growth took place in an unregulated manner with various government agencies and scientific institutions promoting the new technology without any master plan. There was no systematic form of licensing or registration except for those who wanted subsidies and loans. The corporate sector tied up with foreign companies and brought technicians from abroad to undertake semi intensive culture. They also received support from the national financial institutions and the MPEDA. Small farmers on the other hand were left to devise their own farming practices, often with advice only from the feed salesmen of the feed and pharmaceutical companies. Since many of them did not have proper title deeds for their agricultural land, they were unable to access institutional credit. This led them to borrow heavily from the informal credit market at exorbitant interest rates. The technology packages adopted thus ranged from the simple farm pond to the sophisticated integrated units with farms, feed mills and processing plants.

The variations were reflected in the initial investment, which varied from Rs. 12,000 a hectare to Rs. 10,00,000 a hectare. None of these included any effluent treatment equipment.

ENVIRONMENTAL ISSUES

The opposition to shrimp aquaculture stemmed from both environmental and socio-economic problems. The socio-economic problems arose from issues like land alienation; displacement of coastal communities from open access public lands used by them for fish drying, net drying, grazing, subsidence cultivation, etc., Additionally, the conversion of paddy lands, resulting in loss of employment and local level food security and problems of access to the sea for fishermen were also encountered in many areas.

The corporate investors generally chose the beach lands due to the availability of large tracts at low prices although they were aware of the inherent disadvantages for the farming operations. The investments made to compensate for the inherent disadvantages of beach sand, such as sea and ground water pumping apparatus, were the root cause of the negative environmental impacts encountered in these areas particularly by communities living close to these units. Individual farmers made large-scale use of upstream lands, especially paddy fields. The vast majority of them were struggling with low returns from paddy farming and lack of adequate canal water for a second crop. Sensing the opportunity for making quick returns, they shifted en masse to shrimp aquaculture. The debacle after the virus attack left the soil in a highly saline state while the excessive use of antibiotics and chemicals as well as limited water exchange ruined soil productivity. The land is now unfit for both paddy and shrimp culture.

The culture practices of both the corporate units and small farmers were dictated by considerations of short-run profits. These were often risky for the investors themselves and for the environment as well. Some large corporate farms on beach sites adopted culture practices, which required costly high-energy inputs that were propagated as being the most scientific by the foreign controlled feed manufacturing companies. This approach put both the pond ecosystem and the external terrestrial and aquaculture environment under stress. It raised the risk of disease in the ponds and pollution of groundwater outside. Some of the corporate units, which depended on creek-based water sources, went for the second crop when salinity was low. This exposed the crop to virus attacks. As far as the small farms in the upstream lands were concerned, their technology and practices were completely unscientific. Without the use of adequate water exchange mechanisms they used the high-energy imported feeds (swayed by the hard sell of feed suppliers), leading to quick loss of water quality and increase of stress to the shrimp. Thus almost all categories of farms took far too many liberties with nature's assimilative capacity and embarked on unwarranted financial risks, due to both greed and ignorance.

The environmental problems associated with modern shrimp aquaculture are not related to ownership, culture practices or scale of operation. All types and sizes of farms have created environmental problems. However, the nature of the problem and impact are somewhat different. The Andhra Pradesh example is illustrative in this regard. Most of the corporate farms camp up on the sandy beaches of Nellore where land was cheap but the soil porous, leading to stalinization of groundwater and other related social problems. Most of the small farms on the other hand came up in the black cotton soils of Krishna district.

AGRICULTURE VERSUS AQUACULTURE

Large quantities of chemical fertilizers and pesticides are necessary to maintain agricultural productivity at a high level. About 14 million tonnes of chemical fertilizers are used annually in India despite the report by the Indian Council of Agricultural Research that more than 50% of the cultivable area has been affected by soil degradation. More than 100,000 tonnes of insecticides and pesticides are used every year to kill pests and save the crop from disease.

Though much publicity is given to bio-fertilizers and bio-pesticides, it may not be possible to produce them in large quantities to replace the chemical fertilizers and pesticides in the near future. Chemical pesticides kill pests and allow the plant to survive in agriculture whereas in aquaculture the aquatic organisms (fish/shrimp/crab) are killed by chemicals or pesticides. Aquaculture is therefore not only a vital food-producing sector it is at the same time also benign. Compared to the kind of pollution that agriculture causes, aquaculture pollution like human waste is easily treatable. The effluents discharged from shrimp farms are well within the pollution control standards.

NO EVIDENCE

The main chemicals used in aquaculture are lime and chlorine. There is so far no scientific evidence to show that these two chemicals will lead to irreversible soil degradation. It is therefore wrong to say that shrimp culture is a short-lived industry. The aqua farmers in India largely practice extensive farming and there is therefore no need to apply large quantities of lime and chlorine as is the case in Thailand and Taiwan.

Lime and chlorine are in any cases used in the world for hygienic maintenance of surroundings and chlorine even in drinking water. It is an industry of the rich. This is not true. About 99.9 per cent of the shrimp farmers belong to the small-scale sector while there is a small proportion of middle level entrepreneurs. About a dozen companies, which had setup large farms, could not do well. Most of them have ended their operations. However, the contribution of the corporate to developing the basic infrastructure for shrimp farming along with support services such as hatchery seed and feed supply in the beginning as well as the development of roads, communications and electric supply in the rural areas cannot be denied.

ECONOMICS OF BRACKISH WATER CULTURE IN INDIA

Brackish water fish culture has attracted attention as a potentially promising area of fisheries development. It has been estimated that the potential exploitable area of brackish water resources in India is about 1.2-1.4 million hectares.

MANAGERIAL CONSTRAINTS

Conflict in land use–it was found that the agricultural use of land often dominates over brackish water uses. The private landowners as well as the states, agriculture departments discourage the year-round brackish water culture. Water areas are leased out seasonably, which discourages any investment of permanent nature.

OWNERSHIP OF BRACKISH WATER AREAS

Most of the potential brackish water areas are under private ownership. The lands are small and in majority of cases, area for one brackish water farm is under multiple ownership. This leads to problems in creating permanent structures over the area. As a result, the individual landowners jointly lease out the water body, which makes one filtration field. Therefore, it is very difficult to take up IC in these areas. In parts of Andhra Pradesh, large potential areas are under swamps and are property owned by government, which include salt department, revenue and local administrative bodies. Presently, a large part of such areas are being leased out to the fishermen through co-operative societies for capture fisheries (D.V. Reddi, Brackish water farming). The fishermen around these swamp areas are fully dependent on production from the swamps. Conversion of this area for IC will raise several tensions.

POACHING

One of the greatest threats in undertaking brackish water culture is poaching. Unlike any other agricultural crops, where the same is ready for harvesting only for a short -while, fish and prawn are fit for harvesting throughout the period of its culture. It was learnt that in some areas farmers stopped culture because of poaching problems.

LEASING

The private landowners and the state agriculture departments discourage the year round brackish water culture. The water areas are leased out seasonally, which discourages any permanent interest of lease. The long term leasing policy has to be framed for encouraging IC farming.

LAND USE

The agriculture use, and salt production often dominates over brackish water farming. This calls for public policy support measures and needs to be studied in depth keeping in view the relative profitability and employment aspects.

SEED SUPPLY

The commercial side of IC is highly dependent on seed availability. As very little is known in this field, it is recommended that detailed surveys on seed availability may be carried out along the coast. The study should also assess the location and feasibility of rearing farms. The spawners from the sea are available only during season. Therefore, the seed supply from hatcheries is also erratic. In this context, the induction of gonadial maturation and spawning is essential to ensure assured and timely supplies. There is need for intensive research to generically (Hybridization) improve the quality of seed and to reduce erratic fluctuation in quantity. The transportation of seed requires proper planning. The seed requires acclimatization before transport which adds to the cost.

ENGINEERING

The selection of suitable sites for the culture, construction of farms requires knowledge of soil structure, soil properties, flow pattern engineering, etc. At present we have little expertise on coastal farm engineering and it is imperative that we develop the technology immediately so that viable farms could be constructed.

FINANCE

The brackish water culture is an investment-oriented project. The flow of funds has to be considered. The government and the financial institutions should assist in finance through subsidy and loan. The financial institutions should train expertise including for brackish water culture.

TRAINING OF FARMERS

Successful adoption of technology and their wide propagation depends on the extension and training facilities available in the field. Therefore, it is necessary to conduct training of farmers for the development of brackish water culture.

AQUACULTURE–CONTINUING CONTROVERSY

An undisguised craze for striking "aqua gold" runs high in Tamilnadu as seen from the mushrooming of shrimp farms in a haphazard manner, leaving in their wake violent protests from environmentalists and social activists demanding the closure of these farms.

This is the scenario in the state despite the claim of the Chief Minister Ms. Jayalalitha in August 1994, that her government was aware of the environmental and socio-economic problems arising out of the unplanned and indiscriminate setting up of shrimp farms.

The expert committee, constituted by the state government in the wake of an agitation by farm labourers and fishermen against the setting up of shrimp farms on fertile lands, had suggested many a measure to regulate the growth of shrimp farms. But none of the suggestions appears to have been taken note of either by the shrimp farm promoters or the government to surmount the challenges that aquaculture has thrown upto farmers, corporate bodies and other government agencies.

On the other hand, what is now being witnessed is mounting social tension caused by the simmering hatred and distrust between the protagonists and antagonists of shrimp farms? While the promoters insist that, barring a few exceptions, most of the shrimp farms have been setup only on barren and fallow lands on the coastal stretch and that the environmental threat of soil degradation and drinking water sources turning saline is baseless, their opponents assert that there is an unabated spree to buy fertile lands for conversion to shrimp farms, ignoring the dangerous consequences for ecology and biodiversity.

Export of marine products from the state had fetched around Rs. 350 crores last year with shrimps accounting for over Rs. 200 crores and this is expected to double this year.

Environmentalists say that while the sweeping "blue revolution" in the state has ushered in economics prosperity to shrimp farm promoters in general and a few corporate giants in particular, it has wrought an ecological disaster, with the deserticification of fertile lands in villages abutting shrimp farms. This according to them, is a danger to the livelihood of farm labour and fishermen in the coastal belt of Thanjavur and Nagapattinam–Quaid-E milleth (NQM) districts, considered the granary of the state.

They regret that despite a ban on the setting up of shrimp farms in cultivable lands, nearly 1,200 acres of fertile land have so far been taken over by shrimp farm promoters in Sirkazhi taluk of NQM district and in the Thanjavur coastal belt. This is in addition to 5000 acres, already cornered by some big companies and others by offering small and marginal farmers money nearly twenty to thirty times of the land cost.

However, Dr. M. Sakthivel, President of the Aquaculture Foundation of India (AFI) asserts that aquaculture is not a polluting industry like chemical, heavy metal and leather industries. The major inputs in coastal aquaculture are sea water and feed prepared mainly from fish meal, soya meal, oil cakes, minerals and Vitamins. Antibiotics such as oxytetracycline are used in low dosages, which does not have any residual affects either on the shrimps or soil, according to Dr. Sakthivel. He pointed out that since faecal wastes were bio-de-gradable and recycled in the form of nutrients, there was absolutely no pollution by the aquaculture industry. The processed waste of shrimps and other fish was used as an ingredient in the feed industry and the wastewater was treated before being discharged, as per prescribed norms.

The numerous estuaries and creeks, which extended several kilometers in land from the sea, carried high tide saline water and hence the groundwater in these areas are inherently saline. He also refuted the charge that the discharge of untreated effluents in to the sea affected marine life. He said fish get attracted to the point of effluent discharge as it contained a lot of uneaten food. He claimed that aquaculture presented a golden opportunity to usher in a "revolutionary change" in the life of costal villages.

Environmentalists remain unconvinced about claims that aquaculture can be made sustainable without endangering the environment. Developed countries likely USA and Japan can go in for large-scale aquaculture instead of importing shrimps from Asian countries. Only around 3000 tonnes of shrimp are harvested through aquaculture in the U.S. though its coastline is several times longer than that of India.

VIRAL DISEASE

Mr. R. Sambasivam, a former World Bank consultant on aquaculture, who accompanied this report to the site, said the disease was mainly due to the proximity of the effluent channel with the giant inlet pumps drawing seawater. The effluents discharged in to the sea got sucked into the ponds through the inlet pumps, leading to the avoidable destruction of shrimps. The promoters of the farm had subsequently rectified this blunder.

The disease, according to Mr. Sambasivam is not widespread as made out to be since many farms of 20 to 30 acres area along the coast, have had good harvests. He claimed that some of the shrimp farms had ignored the prescribed norms leading to heavy losses. Mr. Sambasivam, who is setting up a shrimp farm at Karanguda near Peravurani, says that every farm should have a senior marine biologist and a couple of junior technicians to check the water quality, oxygen content and ensure that effluents did not mix with the intake water. The shrimp farms had come up on lands, which had remained fallow for several decades. Some stretches had been saltpans once. Hence the propaganda that cultivable lands were been taken over for agriculture was nothing but a canard, he argued.

Dr. P.V. Thomas, managing partner of the Pulikkal aquaculture farm at Vadakupogainallur near Nagapattinam, pointed out that diseases could spread from contaminated water sources and infected shrimp seed. Since the local shrimp feed was not of good quality, he imported feed from Singapore. Some times the diseases in shrimp were caused by the seepage of chemical fertilizers applied in adjacent paddy fields. The reported virus attack on shrimp farms in coastal Andhra Pradesh could be due to the adoption of intensive farming. "We must learn from the experience of countries like Taiwan and Bangladesh, which suffered due to intensive shrimp farming", Mr. Thomas said.

Dr. M. Sakthivel, President of the Aquaculture Foundation of India (AFI), agrees that the virus affecting shrimps has become a serious problem in many parts of the world. However, Thailand is the only country, where the production of shrimps has shown an annual increase. Shrimp farms in that country follow a control system to maintain the quality of water by treating both effluents and the reservoir water. Some are of the opinion that it may be difficult to control this new virus by any chemical treatment. It is also felt that the sudden change in climatic conditions with low temperature, has provided a climate conducive for this virus.

Shrimp farm promoters should ensure that effluents are treated before discharge and go in for extensive farming with low stocking density. Adequate care is required to stock only healthy fry in the ponds. Weak frys supplied by some companies during a heavy demand period may have contributed to the spread of the disease, says Dr. Sakthivel.

According to Dr. K. Alagarswami, Director Central Institute of Brackish Water Aquaculture, Madras, water quality management is critical for aquaculture production. It includes all physical, chemical and biological factors, which influence the survival, growth and production of fish in the ponds.

Water quality is environment related and inputs such as liming for sanitation and correction of hydrogen in concentration, fertilization stocking and feeding interact with the pond environment. Aquaculture has a self-polluting affect due to the accumulation of metabolites, which can be prevented only through proper water quality management. An overdose of shrimp farming in Taiwan led to disastrous consequences, Mr. Alagarswami said. Aquaculture experts say that intensive shrimp farming is based on a dense stocking rate and over crowding, which induces stress problems and increases susceptibility to diseases. Over crowding leads to poor water quality due to decreased oxygen level, accumulation of metabolic products and excreta, rapid growth and transmission of noxious parasites, micro-organisms and pathogens.

Aquaculture interacts with the environment, by using the resources and causing environmental changes. The bio-systems under aquaculture acquire a complex phase due to man's interventions wherein the limits of the inherent carrying capacity of the bio-systems could be put under extreme stress through intensive farming. Generally speaking there have been substantial socio-economic benefits arising from the expansion of aquaculture. These benefits include increased income, employment, foreign exchange earning and improved nutrition. Nevertheless, in several areas environmental degradation has occurred, the extent of which is directly related to the intensity of man's interventions. Aquaculture is competing for land and water resource, which in some cases resulted in conflicts with other resource users. Thus, there is a growing concern about the environmental implications of aquaculture development in the country.

In some cases environmental problems have resulted from conversion of wetland habitats, nutrient and organic and waste discharges, introduction of exotic fishes, chemical uses as well as from deterioration of water quality and decreasing availability of suitable sites for aquaculture. Environmental management of aquaculture development and its promotion are challenging tasks. Unfortunately, there is lack of adequate information and data related to adverse environmental effects of aquaculture in developing countries. Whatever information is available on the subject from temperate countries in most cases cannot be used to predict adverse environmental effect of aquaculture practices in tropical environment. Moreover, much of the information so far gathered on the potential adverse effects of aquaculture are still of speculative nature and are not borne out by scientific evidence. Now that for a certain period the time series data has become available, the lessons learnt would be of use in deciding the future approach.

There are several factors, which influence the environmental compatibility of aquaculture. These are, site selection, layout of the farm and water availability, species selected for aquaculture, culture method, operational procedures, production levels, skill, technology standards, legal status, economic viability and general coordination in over all management.

Based on the current information the key areas of ecological concerns could be visualized. Many aquaculture operations result in the release of metabolic waste products and unconsumed food into the aquatic environment degrading both water and bottom sediments. The release of soluble inorganic nutrients such as nitrogen and phosphorous could cause hypernutrification possibly followed by eutrophication of a water body. The resulting algal blooms may be fatally harmful to the farmed stock. Organic enrichment of the benthic bio-system may result in increased oxygen consumption by the sediments. These could cause in extrement cases,release of carbon dioxide, methane, and hydrogen sulphide etc., and enhanced demineralization of organic nitrogen and reduction of biomass.

Use of fertilizers and feeds will alter water and sediment in ponds and adjacent waters. Fertilizers such as triple–super phosphate, urea, cow dung, chicken manures and rice bran, which are used to promote growth of food organisms may contribute to nutrient and organic loads in the form of metabolites such as ammonia, urea, carbon dioxide and particulate matter which may result in build up of anoxic sediments and algal blooms. Potential ecological problems related to nutrients and organic enrichments in culture operations could occur with semi intensive or more likely with intensive aquaculture of carnivorous cases where provision of feed is essential. Nutrient and organic waste in dissolved or particulate forms from unconsumed food and excreta are generally found in the form of increased suspended solids, B.O.D., C.O.D., carbon, nitrogen and phosphorus. Very little quantitative data is available on these aspects from tropical world. However, these aspects affect the economics of aquaculture operations through enhanced cost of water replenishments and aeration.

A variety of chemicals are used in aquaculture, which include therapeutants, disinfectants, anesthetics, vaccines, flesh pigments, Harmone and growth promoters to control predators, to prevent and control diseases and parasites and to alter the sex, production viability and growth of culture organisms. Over use of antibiotics may generate direct resistance in pathogens such as vibro and pose a risk of transfer of drug resistance to human pathogens. Abuse of antibiotics in Taiwanese hatcheries is a known example.

AQUACULTURE DEVELOPMENT AND SUSTAINABLE ENVIRONMENT

Human population pressure in combination with the expansion and intensification of industry and agriculture causes direct impacts on development of aquaculture. It is also recognized that simultaneously aquaculture causes impacts on other sectoral activities, and also compete with them in sharing of the limited resources. In spite of this, global aquaculture has developed by leaps and bounds, especially in the last two decades. Global aquaculture production of farmed fish (edible "fish and shell fish" according to FAO terminology, FAO, 1996) has increased by 244%, from 7.72 million metric tonnes in 1985 to 18.86 million tonnes in 1994, the corresponding increase in value was 318% from 10.57 billion US dollars to 33.63 billion dollars.

The booming economics of aquaculture and increased socio-economic benefits, such as increase in employment and social well being, concommittment with the increase in the extent and intensity of aquaculture, have created several problems as well especially those of a deteriorating environment, owing to worsening water soil quality, and also due to incursions by aquaculture to the other sectoral activities, such as agriculture, capture fisheries, forestry, public health, tourism, housing etc. the impacts have been two fold, one affecting aquaculture itself by auto pollution and consequent outbreak of diseases leading to crop failures and collapses eventually. The first such national complete collapse in shrimp culture was that of Taiwan (Lin, 1989), followed by partial collapses of cultured shrimp production in China, Indonesia and Thailand, (FAO/NACA, 1995) and now in India. Owing to the lucrative trade value shrimp culture expansion and production increases were dramatic causing collapses of the system and impacts to other sectors, resulting in several complex social problems and litigation at the national level in India, still awaiting legal settlement to decide on the directions Indian coastal aquaculture will take.

GROWTH OF AQUA INDUSTRIES

The global significance of aquaculture can be understood better if we consider that it contributes nearly 22% of the 72 million tonnes of global supply of food fish. The contribution of aquaculture to food fish is even more significant in the case of Asia. China has been the traditional world leader in aquaculture and contributes nearly 50% of the world's production while India, with 10%, is the second largest aquaculture producer.

The modern shrimp aquaculture farms that have come up in recent years are entirely different. These farms are based on the constructions of farms, pumping in brackish water from a suitable source (the sea, brackish water creeks or even canals carrying brackish water), stocking the ponds with shrimp seed (harvested from the wild or produced in hatcheries), feeding the shrimp (with locally formulated feeds with oil cake, fish waste, etc., or industrially produced feed from the market), and subsequently harvesting it after a few months when the growth is adequate.

The crucial parameter in these operations is the level of stocking of shrimp seed in a unit area–the stocking intensity. The culture practices are widely classified as extensive, modify extensive, semi intensive and intensive with the stocking density ranging from 20,000 shrimp seed per hectare to 350,000 per hectare across the range. In general, one can say that increases in stocking intensity imply increases in investment and operating costs. It is also accompanied by greater water exchange brackish and fresh water are pumped into compensate for the releases into the environment of pond water contaminated with feed residues and other organic wastes. Increases in stocking intensity also bring with it the heightened risk of disease and hence the use of drugs and chemicals to combat the problem. Obviously, increased intensity leads to enhanced physical productivity and profits, if unaffected by disease. Increased intensity also reduces the land requirements.

ENVIRONMENTAL ISSUES

The opposition to shrimp aquaculture stemmed from both environmental and socio-economic problems. The socio-economic problems arise from issues like land alienation; displacement of coastal communities from open access pubic lands used by them for fish drying, net drying, grazing, subsistence cultivation, etc. Additionally, the conversion of paddy lands, resulting in loss of employment in local level food security and problems of access to the sea for fishermen where also encountered in many areas.

LOCATION OR SITE SELECTION

The corporate investors generally chose the beach lands due to the availability of large tracts at low prices although they were aware of the inherent disadvantages for the farming operations. The investments made to compensate for the inherent disadvantages of beach sand, such as sea and ground water pumping apparatus, where the root cause of the negative environmental impacts encountered in these areas particularly by communities living close to these units. Individual farmers made large-scale use of upstream lands, especially paddy fields. The vast majority of them were struggling with low returns from paddy farming and lack of adequate canal water for a second crop. Sensing the opportunity for making quick returns, they shifted en masse to shrimp aquaculture. The debacle after the virus attack left the soil in a highly saline state while the excessive use of antibiotics and chemicals as well as limited water exchange ruined soil productivity. The land is now unfit for both paddy and shrimp culture.

The culture practice of both the corporate units and small farmers were dictated by considerations of short run profits. These were often risky for the investors themselves and for the environment as well. Some large corporate farms on beach sites adopted culture practices, which required costly high-energy inputs that were propagated as being the most "scientific" by the foreign control feed manufacturing companies. This approach put both the pond ecosystem and the external terrestrial and aquaculture environment under stress. It raised the risk of disease in the ponds and pollution and ground water outside. Some of the corporate units, which depended on creek-based water sources, went for the second crop when salinity was low. This exposed the crop to virus attacks.

As far as the small farms in the upstream lands were concerned, their technology and practices were completely unscientific. Without the use of adequate water exchange mechanisms they used the high-energy imported feeds (swayed by the hard sell of feed suppliers), leading to quick loss of water quality and increase of stress to the shrimp. Thus almost all categories of farms took far too many liberties with natures assimilative capacity and embarked on unwarranted financial risks, due to both greed and ignorance.

The environmental problems associated with modern shrimp aquaculture are not related to ownership, culture practice or scale of operations. All types and size of farms have created environmental problems.

SALTWATER SEEPAGE

In coastal aquaculture seepage of saltwater into from the shrimp farms into the neighbouring agricultural fields and the drinking water wells has become a controversial issue. What is the reality?

The coastal area is invariably saline because of its proximity to the sea, creeks and estuaries. Every day, for centuries, the high tide saline water has been carried in to the interior through a network of creeks and canals which from the sea face stretch from a few Kms. In Tamilnadu upto 290 KM in West Bengal. Therefore, the coastal zone is not a preferred area for agricultural and in some coastal areas that have been reclaimed for rice cultivation the yields have been very low because of the salt-water ingress. Other large tracts have been laying follow for decades. Thousands of acres of land are lying ideal in several states with out being put to any use.

The incidence of salt-water seepage has been exaggerated as if all of agriculture and all the drinking water wells along India's coastline have been affected by aquaculture. The total area affected by saltwater seepage is insignificant. Moreover, the so-called damage should be set off against the large quantity of food that aquaculture can produce. Just for this reason–which can in case by easily tackled–one should not attempt to sabotage this sector. Out of 1.4 million hectares available in the country aquaculture has developed on only 10% now 7% of the area. Of this area–1,00,000 ha–the productive agricultural land which is next to the aquaculture farms is not even 2% or 2,000 ha. And out of these 2000 ha the land, which is really affected by saltwater seepage, is negligible.

As long as costal aquaculture is restricted to the shores, saltwater seepage and salinisation are not serious problems. It is when the farms are set up more than 500 m from the high tide line that the problem of saltwater seepage can become severe.

The population of drinking water wells should also be examined similarly. There are aquifers in selected pockets along the coastline and no survey has been conducted to assess the number, location and size of these aquifers, the quantity of fresh water available during the year, its quality, etc. based on a few complaints a picture has been created as if all the drinking water wells along the coast line have become saline due to coastal aquaculture.

According to the National Environmental Engineering Research Institute, there is no damage to the drinking water sources (see table). Hence the allegation of water pollution is only a bogey raised by the anti-aquaculturists and the media. However, for a rational approach to aquaculture, certain questions should be asked.

Should villagers in the coastal area be forever dependent on open wells and tanks for their drinking water? Should we not provide closed water supply systems to all coastal villages? Should we leave a large potential unused just because of the salinisation problem in one or two open wells in a village of 50 to 100 families? What on the other hand what will be the return and benefits that will accrue to the villagers and the country as a whole if the area is utilized for aquaculture along with all infrastructural development including potable water supply to the villages?

OVER EXPLOITATION

In general, fisher folk dominate the costal villages. Their catch is going down day by day due to over exploitation. Yet no development plan has been executed so far for improving the living conditions of the coastal population. Other than aquaculture does the fisher folk have any other potential source of alternative livelihood? Under these circumstances the government should come forward with a very positive approach to support coastal aquaculture.

TEETHING PROBLEMS

A new industry always has many teething problems and the problems that aquaculture faces today are no different. If there are genuine problems of saltwater seepage and salinisation of drinking water wells and agricultural lands in the neighbourhood then costal aquaculture should not be practiced in such areas. If still it is practiced in such tracts, the aquaculture farmers should then take adequate steps to prevent saltwater seepage by creating a buffer zone with clay blanketing.

The government should also come forward to create this kind of buffer zone by providing land, canals, etc. for the peaceful coexistence of fishermen, shrimp framers, rice farmers and eco-tourism. The model created in Kung Krabean Bay of Thailand should be adopted in India as well. What is required today is to follow the principle of zonal demarcation. The principle of zonal demarcation should yield a location, specific community master plan so that there is no clash of interest for sharing nature's wealth given.

OTHER CRITICISMS OF AQUACULTURE

- It affects marine life. This is not true. Effluents from shrimp farms increase the productivity of coastal waters. For example, the biological production and standing stock of lagoon fauna in Kung Krabean Bay in Thailand has increased many times over and the fishermen have gained by a two to three–fold increase in their incomes.
- It destroys mangroves and casuarinas. This is an exaggeration. Most of the destruction happened long ago

when land was reclaimed for agriculture, industries and urbanization. The damage done by aquaculture has been negligible. According to the remote sensing surveys, the mangrove area in Andhra Pradesh has actually grown in those areas where shrimp farming has developed the most. If there is destruction of mangroves by the aqua farmers they should carry out a replantation programme for eco-regeneration.

- It reduces the access of fish workers to the sea. This too is an exaggerated criticism. If there is no access to the sea for fishermen then a pathway should be provided.
- It increases unemployment among rural women. This is not true. On the other hand, aquaculture has put a lot of wasteland to use and thereby generated new avenue of employment for men and women. The average labour requirement for rice cultivation is about 180 labour days per crop. Whereas aquaculture requires about 600 days per crop. Thus, aquaculture has not only created additional employment but also increased the income of the labour force. An acute shortage of labour is actually being experienced today in the coastal areas and labourers are being brought from the hinterlands.
- It causes irreverisible damage to the land. This is an imaginary fear. A few non-govermental orgainsations in Tamilnadu have made this criticism without any scientific evidence. They cite the experience of one particular area in Thailand where shrimp farming was practiced on an intensive scale and abandoned for a while due to disease.

The NGOs are probably not aware that the same area is now being used again partly for aquaculture and partly for agriculture. Therefore, there is no question of irreversible damage to the land due to shrimp farming.

AQUACULTURE WASTES AND ITS MANAGEMENT

Though the world wide expansion of aquaculture is making an important contribution to the global supply of aquatics products. But such developments are putting pressure on natural resources such as water and land. It is an irony that the technology relating to blue revolution is advancing, the traditional values are being jeopardized and numerous issues like destruction of mangroves, conversion of agricultural lands to aqua farms, land and water pollution ecological imbalance, disease threats etc. have cropped up in all coastal states. The large amounts of organic and inorganic substances such as food waste and fish feces discharged from intensive aquaculture farms continually accumulate and contaminate the environment. The types of wastes produced in aquaculture farms are basically similar, however, there are differences in the quality and quantity of components depending on the species cultured and the cultured practices adopted.

MANAGEMENT OF AQUACULTURE WASTE

The pollution from the aquaculture waste is considerably that of domestic waste or industrial wastewater. However, effluents produced during pond cleaning has a much greater pollution potential. The release of effluents rich in organic matter, can be expected to result in siltation and changes in productivity and community structure of benthic organisms. Because of these conflicts have arisen between proponents of aquaculture and other users of inland and coastal waters. There is so much of complaint against aquaculture for causing human health hazard, salinisation of ground water, salinisation of marginal paddy field making it unsuitable for agriculture etc. in such cases no one can say that pollution due to aquaculture is a mere illusion though the effect is less than that of other industries.

So, to overcome such situations, there is urgent need to go for environmental friendly aquaculture. Measures, which should be followed, to reduce the aquaculture waste and also help in mitigating or avoiding public health risk from aquaculture development are listed below.

The effluents from the aquaculture farm should be properly treated before discharging to the open water to prevent adverse effects on other water users. In many countries it has become mandatory to have a wastewater treatment pond in aquaculture farms. The aquaculture waste can be treated by physical,

Most extreme examples are quoted in coastal aquaculture development such as saltwater seepage, mangrove destruction, conversion of agri land for aquaculture and others to mislead the public by environmental activists. When compared to the enormous positive effects that coastal aquaculture has created visibly in rural areas, the extent of damage if any, is to be scientifically analyzed. Based on a few stray incidents of saltwater seepage in certain pockets of the costal area, a conclusion has been drawn that saltwater seepage damages agricultural crops and drinking water wells all over the coastal area. When we don't have basic data on groundwater aquifers, the extremists quote that entire aquifer along the coastline of India is damaged. Should we not have the patience and wisdom to conduct survey and collect all data required for verifying the facts as per ground realities before we come to such radical conclusion? The irony is that the environmental activists do not talk about the vast destruction of a productive ecosystem in the coastal areas by reclaiming potential aquaculture land from unpredictable rice farming due to unavailability and/or inadequate availability of fresh water. Whatever damage done to the original ecosystem, e.g., mangrove destruction in the past to develop rice cultivation, is attributed illogically to coastal aquaculture, which is of recent origin in a country like India. The activists play the game very successfully to mislead public and project misconception about coastal aquaculture the challenge before us is to wipe out this false propaganda of the activists and misconception of the public about coastal aquaculture by placing all facts and figures that happened during the last decade.

6

POLICIES FOR SUSTAINABLE AQUACULTURE

ENVIRONMENTAL POLICIES FOR SUSTAINABLE AQUACULTURE

Aquaculture which is one of the recent development in the upliftment of the Indian economy is under the shadow of agriculture, and it does not figure anywhere in the classification of land and water resource and their use. Hence, aquaculture is not given any priority in land use planning or water resources management. The use of irrigation systems, village tanks and reservoirs for aquaculturists is blocked by the absence of integrated development and planning. The entire coastal aquaculture is suffering for want of inclusion of aquaculture in the classification of land. This makes farms of the agricultural and allied sectors to go compulsorily only for unproductive agriculture in the saline soil which is otherwise a "gold mine" for coastal aquaculture with potential to produce tonnes of valuable nutritious shrimp as food of much higher economic value. Productive aquaculture land has been converted long ago for various uses before we could realize the value of aquaculture. When the value and importance of aquaculture are realized now as a vital sector for health food production there is no reason to allow the continuance/ conversion of potential aquaculture land for agriculture or other purposes. At the same time there should be a provision to put back the reclaimed coastal land (which is otherwise classified under agriculture) for coastal aquaculture. Any further construction of saltwater barrier, which alters the entire coastal ecosystem should be stopped. Instead of doing it, saltwater irrigation system in the declared area after a survey should be developed and legalized to promote eco friendly coastal aquaculture. Coastal aquaculture must be accepted and legally recognized as a legitimate user of water and should be treated as a water front activity.

There is no legal provision and procedure to allot water bodies in the coastal area for sea farming which is the largest untapped potential in India. The aquaculture will, which is being introduced, covers only coastal aquaculture on land. Therefore why need a comprehensive bill/law covering aquaculture in fresh water, brackish water in marine ecosystem. In the coastal management plan of all maritime states, aquaculture should be given priority and well integrated in the system. The existing environment production Act 1986 and the notification of Feb. 1991 should be properly abounded to accommodate and protect the interest of coastal aquaculture developed in India.

Most extreme examples are quoted in coastal aquaculture development such as saltwater seepage, mangrove destruction, conversion of agriculture land for aquaculture and others to mislead the public by environmental activists. When compared to the enormous positive effects that coastal aquaculture have created visibly in rural areas, the extent of damage if any, is to be scientifically analyzed. Based on a few stray incidents of saltwater seepage in certain pockets of the costal area, a conclusion has been drawn that saltwater seepage damages agricultural crops and drinking water wells all over the coastal area. When we don't have basic data on groundwater aquifers, the extremists quote that entire aquifer along the coastline of India is damaged. Should we not have the patience and wisdom to conduct survey and collect all data required verifying the facts as per ground realities before we come to such radical conclusion? The irony is that the environmental activists do not talk about the vast destruction of a productive ecosystem in the coastal areas by reclaiming potential aquaculture land from unpredictable rice farming due to unavailability and/or inadequate availability of fresh water. Whatever damage done to the original ecosystem, e.g., mangrove destruction in the past to develop rice cultivation, is attributed illogically to coastal aquaculture, which is of recent origin in a country like India. The activists play the game very successfully to mislead public and project misconception about coastal aquaculture the challenge before us is to wipe out this false propaganda of the activists and misconception of the public about coastal aquaculture by placing all facts and figures that happened during the last decade.

Environmental degradation manifests itself through bio-indicators, but it is not easily understood by many stakeholders. There are many reasons for this. Firstly, the boundaries of adverse environmental impacts are not easy to demarcate as they do not respect the jurisdiction of states or State pollution control boards (SPCBs). It is also difficult to assess the extent of the damage. Another major problem for the regulatory agencies is sourcing mixed effluents and emissions. Thus, the easy way out for the resource-constrained government agencies is to be a "stock holder" like others, instead of talking proactive steps to undo the damage.

Technology or market forces do not favour the environment. Hence, to save the environment from degradation, what are needed policy interventions. Physically this would mean getting priorities organized. It would mean choosing reduced industrial effluents, for instance, at the source itself rather than encourage construction of common effluent treatment plants and disposal facilities.

The age-old conflict between development and environment, which was acknowledged by the west, is yet to be understood in India. Economists are often looked upon suspiciously by environmentalists. Micro–economic approaches have never been thought of one such approach is the safe minimum standard, which explicitly states that we should avoid irreversible environmental damage unless the social cost of under taking the project is infinity.

Defining short-term measures therefore becomes an exercise in proactive environmental management, using micro economic approaches as close as possible to the scene of environmental impact. To begin with, we should use available laws and systems, suitable economic models and applicable technology. It will involve hands on training and empowering the directly affected stockholders.

ALLOTMENT OF LAND FOR AQUACULTURE BY GOVERNMENT

Allotment of land for aquaculture should be made only as per the recommendations of the State High level committee. Fisheries department should prepare the master plan for each block of land so that the water in-let and drainage facilities could be scientifically planned allowing access to sea for their facilities for big and medium entry and providing common facilities for small scale and private sectors allotters. Fisheries department should also take into account the private lands surrounded by Government poramboke lands and vice-versa while preparing these master plan.

It was decided that for small-scale and private sector allottees/lease rent may be waived for the first year. Waiver in II year may be decided by the district level committee by the District Collector and representatives of the fisheries department and fisheries institutions.

It was considered advisable to revise the lease rent periodically, meet in 5 years and agreed to collect the rent twice in a year conveniently with the harvest and the sale of prawns.

CONVERSION OF AGRICULTURAL LANDS

It is generally considered that productive agricultural land is the most ideal land for aquaculture. But large scale conversion of such land into aquafarms leads to hypernitrification that in turn leads to high production of phytoplankton affecting the standing crop. High levels of nutrients can cause blooms of toxic species which may result in mass mortality of the cultured species. Increased levels of dissolved organic matter cause an increase in the numbers of micro organisms, especially bacteria. Growth of filamentous algae and macrophytes may also occur. In marine environment, changes in the natural production of phytoplankton and macro algae have been recognised in the vicinity of farms, where there is vigorous flushing. Besides stimulation of primary production, changes may occur in the species composition and abandance of phytoplankton and in increased macrophyte growth.

The nature of fauna of the receiving water is influenced by the dissolved oxygen (DO) concentration, nature of substrate and availability of food in aquafarm effluents. It is a common practice to convert agricultural land and land under salt production, into coastal aquaculture units. Conversion of agricultural farms and salt making lands had been rampant in fragile coastal areas of Andhra Pradesh, Tamilnadu and Pondicherry.

STATE REGULATION

If fisheries arises from the common property/open access nature of the resource without property rights, individual fishermen have no incentive to consider the opportunity cost of harvesting (i.e., the opportunity cost of harvesting value of the productive capacity of the stock). Instead, fishermen tend to harvest as much and as fast as they can as long as expected net return is positive. Under these conditions, resource depletion can occur. The task facing the fishery manager is the promulgation of regulations designed to ensure continued harvests and, if possible, to enhance the value of those harvests. Most important, the fishery manager does not want to promulgate regulations that are inconsistent with optimal harvest strategies.

Bioeconomic models and optimal control theory can be used by fishery managers to help attain these goals. With a specified objective (such as maximizing net revenue) and a specified control variable, or regulatory device (such as the season opening date), optimal control theory can solve for the optimal resource harvest over time and the optimal regulation. The procedure requires a bioeconomic model of the fishery. Important components include the objective function, the price function, the fish production function, the cost function, and functions describing the population dynamics of the resource stock. A number of recent works have advanced theoretical optimal control models(for example, Clark; Huang, Vertinsky, and Wilimoiovsky; Strand and Hueth; Clark and Munro; Levhari, Michener and Mirman; Conrad and Castro), but there are few examples of successful applications to fishery problems.

A general dynamic harvesting model to determine when to open the harvest season for a seasonal fishery is presented here. The model is applied to the North Carolina bay scallop fishery. Results show that even with data limitations, this analysis makes a strong case for significant returns to a change in traditional management of the fisheries.

THE ECONOMICS OF LANDSCAPE CONSERVATION: MARKET FAILURE AND THE NEED FOR EFFICIENT POLICY

The economic behaviour of farmers and other land users is guided by the prices of those inputs and outputs they buy or sell in the market. Thus, for example when a decision on milk output is to be made, market prices provide information enabling a farmer to compare the marginal value of milk output with it marginal cost and to select the optimal output level accordingly. However, other outputs of farming are not traded in the market and thus command no market price. A good example is given by landscape attributes that depend on particular styles of farming for their production and maintenance. Landscape attributes are typically non-excludable public goods. Thus, farmers are prevented from charging others for the enjoyment of these attributes. On the other hand, society as a whole has no well-defined and enforceable rights over landscape attributes, and thus farmers are not charged for degrading the landscape.

The fact of landscape attributes being unpriced does not mean they have no effect on other people's welfare. It means, however, that, more often than not, farmers will not take this external effect on others' welfare into account. Thus, in particular price, technology or policy contexts, farmers are led to change management in ways that cause significant negative effect on others' welfare with no regard for all for these effects. For example, high labour costs may put an end to the upkeep of traditional structures such as stone walls or terraced fields, with the attendant process of decay having a negative effect on visitors to the countryside. Along the same lines, prices and policy may lead farmers to intensify fertilizer use, which reduces socially-valued flower diversity in meadows.

The above examples show that levels of landscape attributes, and hence the welfare of those valuing these attributes, are an unintended side effect of management decisions taken by farmers and other land users. Economists call this type of unintended side effect on others' welfare an externality. Externalities can be positive or negative according to the sign of the external effect on welfare. Thus, the upkeep of traditional structures is an example of a positive externality of some farming systems; likewise, grassland ploughing for conservation into arable may represent a negative externality.

A well-known theorem of neoclassical welfare economics states that ,within a competitive market and assuming perfect information, choices by rational individuals will lead to a particular type of social optimum: the Pareto Optimum. The Pareto Optimum is a situation where nobody can be made better off without making someone else worse off (this is seen as an optimal situation because there are no more opportunities left for unequivocal improvements in resource allocation: all possible improvements for someone will leave others worse off). However, in the presence of externalities this theorem does not hold. Therefore, landscape externalities are a source of market failure: too high levels of negatively valued attributes and too small levels of positively valued ones(with respect to socially optimal levels) will be produced by the market if this is left to act by itself. Sometimes, as is well illustrated by the negative environmental effects of agricultural policy, the problem is not only one of market failure but one of policy failure as well. Market and policy failures provide a rationale for government to intervene in the supply of landscape attributes.

PIGOUVIAN PARADOX

One of the core principles of sustainable development is the "Polluter Pays" Principle. This recognizes that the polluter should pay for any environmental damage created. The

Polluter Pays Principle was first widely discussed in the United Nations Conference on Environment and Development held in Rio de Janeiro, Brazil in June 1992. All the representatives of the countries and nations endorsed the principle, which became a part of the Rio Declaration.

"National authorities should promote the internalization of environmental costs and the use of economic instruments, taking into account the approach that the polluter should, in principle, bear the cost of pollution (Rio Declaration, Principle 16)".

The principle of allowing pollution to occur, but taxing it, derives from A C Pigou, the famous economist. In 1932, he argued that pollution taxes would force offending industries to "internalize" the costs they were imposing on others. It is an approach, which contrasts with banning pollution outright or allowing it within certain limits. The merit of taxation is that firms will dare to pollute only if the benefits outweigh the costs. The tax will also generate revenue that can be used to compensate those who suffer.

A polluter is someone who directly or indirectly damages the environment or one who creates conditions leading to such damage. Pollution is the imposition of a harmful waste product or emission on to the person or property of another without that person's consent; it is a "trespass under the principles of common law. If the trespass is so minor that it creates no impact or inconvenience for the property owner, it will normally be tolerated. Otherwise, it will likely result in legal action of some kind.

Coastal aquaculture continues to grow rapidly in many parts of the world. Possible environmental and social impacts from costal aquaculture have been profusely documented and could be summed up as nutrient enrichment, habitat loss and change and impacts on wild fin and shellfish populations.

Application of the Polluter Pays Principle in shrimp farming is complex as it deals largely with ecological systems, the understanding of which will always include scientific uncertainty. Many of the impacts of coastal aquaculture are uncertain and also difficult to quantify. However, such uncertainty cannot be an excuse to avoid responsible ecological decision-making–as failing to act today might force significant social and ecological costs tomorrow.

In the context of shrimp farming the Polluter Pays Principle needs to be better understood and, ultimately, to be reinstated under institutional arrangements that make it effective and fair. The following paragraphs explain some of the options that could be exercised to implement the Polluter Pays Principle in shrimp farming in the country.

ENVIRONMENTAL LIABILITY

Environmental liability is a way of implementing the Polluter Pays Principle. The application of this method will encourage the various parties concerned to take more precaution and will reduce pollution. India does have laws on liability for activities hazardous to the environment, but these laws largely concern damage to human health or property. An environmental liability regime for damage to natural resources is lacking.

On the ground, environmental liability will be effective and cheap to implement only when it is possible to identify clearly the polluter responsible for the damage. It also becomes difficult to implement liability for tackling environmental damage, especially when the damaged natural assets are not privately owned. This is practically impossible with diffuse pollution where many different actors contribute small amounts to the overall problem.

To implement environmental liability, in the first place, anyone who levels allegations of damage (or risk of damage) should provide some reasonable supporting evidence. This also foresees that the operator should be obliged to disclose to the competent authority the relevant data and information to help establish the facts of the case.

For the principle of liability to be effective it is, therefore, essential that:

Polluters must be identifiable;

the damage must be quantifiable;

there must be a link between the polluter and the damage; and

the party liable under an environmental liability regime should be the person performing the activity.

Approaches based on common law damages are difficult to implement and to prove. For example, in most parts of the coastal areas, which are inherently saline, it would be difficult to prove that a particular farm holder is responsible for an observed salinity problem. Similarly, it would be still more complex to apportion pollution damages in a creek due to shrimp waste water given that the runoff from agricultural fields or municipal wastes from upstream sources also contribute to higher levels of nutrients and contaminants.

For restoration of the damage, the situation will differ according to the type of damage: usually soil and water can be decontaminated. Damage to biodiversity might be more complex to restore. In such a situation, the competent authorities should have the choice of restorative measures. When a site that has been damaged cannot be restored on the spot, another site nearby that has an equivalent environmental value for biodiversity could be enhanced. A site located even further away from the damaged site, but which fulfils the same environmental role, could equally be improved.

Insurability is important to ensure that the objectives of an environmental liability regime are attained. However, at the moment, there is no widespread coverage of environmental damage risks in the country. When damage is 'orphaned', ie; the responsible polluter cannot be identified or has no money to pay for the damage, the Government may be required to ensure that the contamination is cleaned up or the damage rectified. It may rely on funding mechanisms set up specifically for this purpose. It is, therefore, essential that the Government put into place "safety nets" to ensure that orphan damages are actually rectified.

One way to adequately implement the Polluter Pays Principle would be to set up an environment restoration fund. Money could be charged from the "polluter" to insure against a likely adverse environmental impact, and returned only if after due time the technology, process or product in question demonstrates that it is reasonably safe. Alternatively, if damage occurs, the fund will be used for environmental restoration, and to pay damages to those who have been harmed. Since the "fund" accrues interest, the "polluter" has an incentive to adopt the good management practices and to demonstrate that the technology, process or product is as safe as possible.

The Polluter Pays Principle is an ideal concept to restrain industries from polluting the environment and its uniform application can encourage rational use and judicious use of environmental resources, especially those in coastal areas, which are impacted by a host of activities.

CONSTITUTION OF INDIA AND ENVIRONMENTAL LAW

In India the right to life, a fundamental right, has been extended to include the right to a healthy environment. The State has a duty to protect and preserve the ecosystem. This is a part of the directive principles of State Policy and it is the duty of the State to apply these principles in making laws. The fundamental right to life has been further expanded to include, inter alia, right to liberty, livelihood, healthy/clean environment or protection against degrading environment The "precautionary Principle" and the "Polluter Pays Principle" have been accepted as part of law of the land. Article 21 of the Constitution of India guarantees protection of life and personal liberty. Articles 48A and 51A(g) of the Constitution are as under:

48A. Protection and improvement of environment and safeguarding of forests and wildlife. The State shall endeavour to protect and improve the environment and to safeguard the forests and wildlife of the country.

51A(g). To protect and improve the natural environment including forests, lakes, rivers and wildlife, and to have compassion for living creatures.

Apart from the constitutional mandate to protect and improve the environment the other most relevant enactments are the Water(Prevention and Control of Pollution) Act, 1974 (The Water Act), The Air(Prevention and Control of Pollution Act, 1981(The Air Act) and the Environment (Protection) Act, 1986. The Water Act, 1974 prohibits the use of streams and wells for disposal of polluting matters and also provides for curbs on outlets and discharge of effluents without obtaining consent from the Central Pollution Control Board. Prosecution and penalties have been provided which include sentence or imprisonment.

'POLLUTER PAYS' PRINCIPLE

The union will probably let another budget go by without applying the polluter pays principle to reduce damage to environment. Pay for the damage if you pollute. Pay more if you pollute more. This, in simple terms, is the polluter pays principle. The Indian government chooses to ignore the message emerging from countries across the world, that makers and users of vehicles must pay the full cost of damage to environment from transportation. European nations are designing fiscal instruments to develop a sustainable environment policy. This European Union (EU) is now using market-based instruments not only to Environmental degradation and pollution are today the most challenging problems before the mankind. The cutting of forests, desertification and erosion of the soil, depletion of natural resources, pollution of lakes, rivers and oceans, accumulation of wastes and hazardous substances are common problems of all the countries in the world. And on top of there are global threats of climate change and depletion of ozone layer. It has become amply clear that a multi-pronged strategy is required to make environmental protection meaningful and tangible.

POLLUTER PAY PRINCIPLE HAVING LEGAL SANCTION

The Supreme Court, in Vellore Citizens Welfare forum Vs Union of India and others(1996), has dealt with the concept of "sustainable development" and has specifically accepted the 'Precautionary Principle and the "Polluter Pays Principle" as part of the environmental laws of the land. The court noted that although the leather industry is a major foreign exchange earner of India and provided employment it does not mean that this industry has the right to destroy the ecology, degrade the environment or create health hazards. The relevant part of the judgement is as under:

"The traditional concept that development and ecology are opposed to each other is no longer acceptable. "Sustainable Development" is the answer. In the international sphere "Sustainable Development" as a concept came to be known for the first time in the Stockholm Declaration of 1972. In the earth Summit held in June 1992 at Rio, world leaders deliberated and chalked out blueprint for the survival of the planet. Among the tangible achievements of the Rio Conference was the adoption of Agenda 21, a programme of action into the next century in areas like poverty, population and pollution. During the two decades from Stockholm to Rio "Sustainable Development" has come to be accepted as a viable concept to eradicate poverty and improve the quality of human life while living within the carrying capacity of supporting ecosystems. "Sustainable Development" as a balancing concept between ecology and development has been accepted as a part of the Customary International Law and that the "Precautionary Principle" and the "Polluter Pays Principle" are essential features of "Sustainable Development".

Thus the Court, invoking the provisions of the Environment (Protection) Act, 1986, ordered the Central Government to establish an authority to deal with the situation created by the tanneries and other polluting industries in the State of Tamilnadu and directed that the authority shall implement precautionary principle and the polluter pays principle, and identify the (1) loss to the ecology/environment; and (2) individuals/families who have suffered because of the pollution, and then determine the compensation to reverse this environmental damage and compensate those who have suffered from the pollution. Further, each tannery in the listed district is subject to a Rupees 10,000 fine, which will be put into an "Environment Protection Fund". This fund will be used to restore the environment and to compensate affected persons. Expert bodies will help frame a scheme to reverse the environmental pollution. All tanneries must set up common effluent treatment plants, or individual pollution control devices, and if they do not, the Superintendent of Police and the Collector/ District Magistrate/Deputy Commissioner in each of the respective districts is authorized to close the plants down. No new industries shall be permitted to be set up within the listed prohibited areas.

"The Polluter Pays Principle" has been held to be a sound principle by the Supreme Court in another case-Indian Council for Enviro-Legal Action Vs Union of India (1996). In this case the Court observed:

"Once the activity carried on is hazardous or inherently dangerous, the person carrying on such activity is liable to make good the loss caused to any other person by his activity, irrespective of the fact whether he took reasonable care while carrying on his activity. The rule is premised upon the very nature of the activity carried on". Consequently, the polluting industries are "absolutely liable to compensate for the harm caused by them to villagers in the affected area, to the soil and to the underground water and hence, they are bound to take all necessary measures to remove sludge and other pollutants lying in the affected areas". The "Polluter Pays Principle" as interpreted by this Court means that the absolute liability for harm to the environment extends not only to compensation for the victims of pollution but also to the cost of restoring the environmental degradation. Remediation of the damaged environment is part of the process of "Sustainable Development" and as such the polluter is liable to pay the cost to the individual sufferers as well as the cost of reversing the damaged ecology.

STRATEGIES

- Develop a broad environment policy and support it with a plan for above 20 years, set mile stones to achieve parameters;
- Internalize environmental considerations in all state policies, plans, programs and projects;
- Establish locally–relevant standards;
- Decentralize monitoring and legal action, centralize technology and expertise support; and
- Implement annual action plans, meet all costs internally and monitor progress on a monthly basis.

THE EARTH SUMMIT 1992

The historic earth summit held in Rio-de-Janeiro (Brazil) came to a close on 14th June 1992. The 178 nations, which participated in it, adopted the Rio declaration on environmental development. The declaration-stated human beings were at the center of concern for sustainable development and set the goal of establishing a new and equitable global partnership through the creation of new levels of co-operation among states, key sector of societies and people.

The development of national law regarding viability and compensation for the victims of pollution and other environmental damage was also clearly spelt out. The 25 principles of Rio declaration embraced the entire gamut of concerns that the world had to urgently contend with to protect the planet. The role of women, youth, and indigenous people in environmental management and development was stressed in the declaration.

ENVIRONMENT ACTION POLICIES, COMMITTEES AND LAWS IN INDIA

- India is one of the few countries in the world that have made specific reference in the construction to the need for environmental protection and improvement.
- The forty-second amendment of constitution 1976 has made it a fundamental duty to protect and improve the natural environment. By clause (g) to article 51A.
- It shall be the duty of every citizen of India to protect and improve the natural environment including forests, lakes, rivers and wild life and to have compassion for living creatures.
- Article 47 of the constitution of India provides for the improvement of public health as one of the duties imposed on the state.
- The aforesaid provisions are wide enough to empower the government to do all the necessary to do buy legislative and administrative action to protect human environment. The state is empowered not only to adopt a policy for the

protection of environment but also to take effective steps to improve polluted environment and to prevent pollution of environment.

NEED FOR LEGAL STATUS OF SUSTAINABLE AQUACULTURE

In recent years, increasing attention is being paid on the environmental problems of the costal areas. The coastal areas contain diverse and productive areas, which are important for human settlements, development and subsistence. More than 50% of the world's population lives with in 60 Km of the shoreline; it is expected that is shoreline population increase substantially in the next 30 years. It is a matter of concern that coastal areas include very rich but most fragile ecosystems, which are being rapidly degraded. It is in this situation shrimp farms began to proliferate in the coastal areas of India in the 1990s. Several coastal countries like Australia, China, France, Israel, Japan, Thailand, UK, USA and others have taken steps for coastal zone management following the 1992 UN Conference on Environment and Development (UNCED). Chapter 17 of Agenda 21 of the above conference emphasizes the need to "provide for an integrated policy and decision making process, including all involved sectors, to promote the compatibility and a balance of uses" and to "apply preventive and precautionary approaches in project planning and implementation, including prior assessment and systematic observation of the impacts of major projects". Therefore, many coastal countries have evolved integrated coastal zone management (ICZM) plans. India too has initiated actions to exercise powers under section 3 (i) and 20 (v) of the environment (protection) Act, 1986 through a legal instrument called the Coastal Regulation Zone (CRZ) Notification. 1991

NEED FOR POLICIES

It is now widely recognized that the major problems in shrimp farming are essentially due to the unregulated growth of the farms, and hence the system as such could not be blamed. Scientific methods and remedies are available for refining the current practices to make them socially and environmentally acceptable. There are evidences from several countries that the shrimp farming is sustainable both economically and ecologically. Evolving appropriate policies and development of sustainable shrimp farms in India is handicapped by the non-availability of quantitative and qualitative scientific data on the factors responsible for degradation of the environment.

POLLUTION CHARGES

Emission charges are used in both Europe and Japan, though more commonly to control water pollution than air pollution (Anderson (1977), Brown and Johnson (1984), Bressers (1988), Vos (1989), Opschoor and Vos (1989) and Sprenger (1989)). Currently effluent charges are being used to control water pollution in France, Italy, Germany, and the Netherlands. In both France and the Netherlands the charges are designed to raise revenue for the purpose of funding activities specifically design to improve water quality. In Germany discharges are required to meet minimum standards of wastewater treatment for a number of defined pollutants. Simultaneously, a fee is levied on every unit of discharge depending on the quantity and noxiousness of the effluent. Discharges meeting or exceeding state of the art effluents standards have to pay only half of the normal rate. The Italian effluent charge system was mainly designed to encourage polluters to achieve provisional effluent standards as soon as possible. The charge is nine times higher for firms that do not meet prescribes standards than for firms that meet them. This charge system was designed only to facilitate the transaction to the prescribed standards so it is scheduled to expire once full complaints has been achieved.

- Economists typically envisage to the types of effluent or emission charges. The first, an efficiency charge, is designed to produce an efficient outcome by forcing the polluter to compensate completely for all damage caused. The second a cost effective charge is designed to achieve a predefined ambient standard at the lowest possible control cost. In practice, few, if any implemented programs fit either of these designs.

- Despite being design mainly to raise revenue, effluent charges have typically improved water quality. Though the improvements in most cases have been small, apparently due to the low level at which the effluent charge rate is set, the Netherlands, with its higher effective rates, reports rather large improvements. Air pollution charges typically have not had much effect on air quality because the rates are too low and in the case of France, most of the revenue is returned to the polluting sources.
- The revenue from charges is typically earmarked for specific environmental purposes rather than contributed to the general revenue as a means of reducing the reliance on taxes that produce more distortions in resource allocation.
- The Swedish tax on heavily polluting vehicles and subsidy for new low polluting vehicles was very successful in introducing low polluting vehicles in to the automobile pollution at a much faster than normal rate. The policy was not revenue natural, however, owing to the success of the programme in altering vehicle choices, the subsidy payments greatly exceeded the tax revenue.

FIRST PRINCIPLES

Assuming all participants are cost minimizers, a "well defined" emissions trading are emission charge system could cost effectively allocate the control responsibility for meeting a predefined pollution target among the various pollution sources despite incomplete information on the control possibilities by the regularity authorities (for the formal demonstration of this preposition (Baumol and Oates, 1975, Montgomery, 1972 and Titenberg, 1985).

Minimization will occur when the marginal cost of control is set equal to the emission reduction credit price or the emission charge. Since all cost minimizing sources would choose to control until their marginal control costs were equal to the same price or charge, marginal control costs would be equalized across all discharge points, precisely the condition required for cost effectiveness.

Emission charges could also sustain a cost effective allocation of the control responsibility for meeting a predefined pollution target, but only if the control authority knew the correct level of the charge to impose or was willing to engage in an iterative trial and error process over time to find correct level. Emissions trading does not face this problem because the price levels is established by the market not the control authority (Titenberg, 1988) .

Economic incentive approaches offer a unique opportunity for regulators to solve a fundamental dilemma. The control authorities desire to allocate the responsibility for control cost effectively is inevitably frustrated by lack of information sufficient to achieve this objective. Economic incentive approaches create a system of incentives in which those who have the best knowledge about control opportunities, the environmental managers for the industries, are encouraged to use that knowledge to achieve environmental objectives at minimum cost. To be consistent with a cost effective allocation of the control responsibility, the policy instruments would have to be defined in different ways for different types of pollutants.

Once the control authority has decided how much pollution of each type will be allowed, it must then decide how to allocate the operating permits among the sources. In theory emission reduction credits could either be auctioned off, with the sources purchasing them from the control authority at the market-clearing price or (as in the US programme) created by the sources as surplus reductions over and above a predetermined set of emission standards.

ECONOMIC INSTRUMENTS

Economic instruments allow pollution targets to be met at the lowest aggregate cost to the polluters but this is not necessarily the lowest cost to society since there are other cost factors. Specifically there is the issue of compliance costs discussed earlier. While some writers have chosen to ignore control costs, assuming that they are invariant between instruments are trivial, this, as discussed below, is not necessarily the case.

ECONOMIC ANALYSIS OF INSTRUMENTS

It is important to distinguish economic instruments as a class of instruments from the economic analysis of instruments. Instrument choice requires an understanding of how instruments achieve their objectives and this is the subject of economic analysis. This analysis is required because neither economic instruments nor command and control instruments are self-policing. Thus with command and control it has to be recognized that people do not necessarily obey the law.

Because they are not self-policing all economic instruments must ultimately be backed by the law. Both monitoring and enforcement of pollution controls entail costs that are collectively termed compliance costs. The incidence of these compliance costs, whether in the first instance they fall on the polluter or the control authority, will depend on the specific details of the instrument. Regardless of the incidence of compliance costs, society has an interest in minimizing their total value since the resources committed to control have an opportunity cost.

POLLUTION TAXES AND SUBSIDIES

A pollution tax is identical to a Pigovian tax except that its rate is set to achieve a predetermined standard and not some presumed social optimum. One way of financing a subsidy on the installation of pollution-control equipment would be to levy a pollution tax and to recycle the revenue to the polluters in the form of a system of grants for the installation of pollution-control equipment. If successful such a tax-subsidy scheme would self–destruct ; the subsidies would fund investment by the polluters that would reduce their future tax liabilities. Even without recycled subsidies, one possible response of the polluter to the levying of a pollution tax would be to invest in pollution-control to reduce tax liability.

POLLUTION CONTROL AS AN ENTRY BARRIER

Markets only ensure economic efficiency if they are competitive. Competitiveness requires that producers are free to enter markets if they perceive opportunities for making profits and to leave markets, to cease production, when the opportunities for profit disappear. Pollution control could be a barrier to entry to a market in certain circumstances. Thus if a pollution control authority meets its targets by subsidizing the existing polluters to install pollution-control equipment a potential new entrant to the industry could be forced to fund the investment in control equipment itself. In this case the potential new entrant would be faced with higher costs than existing producers and thus be placed at a competitive disadvantage. Similarly if targets were met by command and control and existing producers were in aggregate producing as much pollution as the control authority would permit, a potential entrant would be unable to obtain consent. Thus both command and control and subsidies for equipment installation could constitute entry barriers.

POLICY MEASURES FOR AQUACULTURE

1. Aquaculture is a form of agriculture and therefore should be allowed within the CRZ.
2. Activities dependent on the sea-coast should legally operate within the CRZ.
3. National and state exechequer and the banking sector will be severely affected with far reaching consequences if the industry is banned and therefore the industry should be given careful priority to form a sustainable and eco-friendly environment.
4. Aquaculture should continue but with a check on environment degradation. The environmental protection authorities could prioritize their work on environmental quality, environmental impacts, environmental politics and environmental economics. High environmental quality is essential for consumer acceptability and premium market price.
5. The possibilities of creating an environmental value added tax (EVAT) is also on the anvil and the polluters should be made to pay for it if they don't follow the environmental criteria.

6. Legislation should be accompanied by economic disincentives that penalize polluting industries.
7. Appropriate legal and administrative framework to facilitate the development of responsible aquaculture should be established.
8. The country should produce and regularly update aquaculture development strategies and legal measures to ensure that aquaculture development is ecologically sustainable and to allow the rational use of resources shared by aquaculture and other activities.
9. The country should ensure that the livelihoods of local communities, and their access to fishing grounds are not negatively affected by aquaculture developments.
10. The country should establish effective procedures specific to aquaculture to undertake appropriate environmental assessment and social consequences resulting from water extraction, land use, discharge of effluents, use of drugs and chemicals and other aquaculture activities.
11. The country should establish databases and information networks to collect , share and disseminate data related to aquaculture activities to facilitate cooperation on planning for aquaculture development at the national level.
12. Fiscal instruments should be designed to develop sustainable aquaculture policy.
13. Market based instruments should be used to address environmental issues like quantity of wastes discharged, salinization and ground water contamination.
14. Polluters should be made to pay (Polluters tax) based on the level of effluent disposal.

STRATEGIES TO BE ADOPTED

Aquaculture Economics

(a) Economic evaluation of each aquaculture production system to identify economically viable systems.

(b) Economic evaluation of aquaculture inputs, viz. seed, feed, fertilizers etc.,

(c) Study of socio-economic impact of aquaculture.

Prevention of environmental degradation due to aquaculture

(a) Standardization of procedure for environmental impact assessment (EIA)

(b) Carrying out appropriate EIA on mandatory basis before embarking on large aquaculture projects

(c) Standardization of techniques to prevent environmental degradation through effective treatment and management of the farm effluent. Every farm should have an extensive settling tank to receive and retain the effluent over a period of time, after which the supernatant water could be let off into a natural drain or re-used in the farm after further treatment. There should be buffer areas between farms.

(d) Internalise environmental considerations in all state policies, programmes and projects.

PUBLIC OPINION

A developing country like India needs more foreign exchange for importing basic raw materials, advanced technology etc. Export of marine products is also encouraged in order to earn foreign exchange. Shrimps continued to be the largest item realising the highest foreign exchange earning among the marine products. As we have already seen, shrimp culture has been undertaken in many parts of the country, mainly due its lucrative export earnings. Since capture fisheries are unable to supply sufficient volume of shrimps to meet the increasing demand and as a result of the new techniques of producing shrimp seeds in hatcheries, shrimp culture has become an attractive enterprise in many countries including India. But this shrimp culture is creating some side effects also, as already seen.

The public opinion about the closure of existing aquafarms and the pollution problems are interdependent. Moreover opinion of the people regarding the closure of the aquafarm is divided. A section of the public has said that these farms must be closed. Another section has said that aquaculture is the panaecea for all the ills there and aquaculture has to be encouraged for promoting the economic welfare in the region.

There is no linear relationship between public opinion on the future of farms and the benefits the public receive, their education level and the pollution problems.

Analysis of various factors involved indicates that the benefits the people receive from aquafarms is the most important factor.

It is found that more than 35 per cent of the employees working in the aquafarms are educated. It is found that 75 per cent of the employees in the aquafarms are getting a salary of Rs. 1000/- and above each, per month.

Many of the employees (83 per cent) have felt that they have got increased wages in aquafarms.

Facilities like roads, electricity and water supply have improved according to 28 and 25 employees respectively.

More than 60 per cent of the general public feel that they get better value for their lands.

About 30% of the general public feel that they have got better road facilities due to the development of shrimp industry.

Among the disadvantages experienced by the general public, the reduction of job opportunities in agriculture is given importance by most of the respondents (60 per cent). Likewise about 42 per cent of them have revealed their concern about the conversion of agricultural lands into aquafarms.

It is understood that the number of respondents who are happy about the creation of job opportunties in aquafarms is less than the number of respondents who have stated the reduction of jobs in agricultural farms.

Many have stated that the aquafarms should be allowed to continue, but at the same time measures should be taken to check pollution.

Foreign exchange earnings from the export of marine products in general and from the export of shrimps in particular have increased over the years.

The share of shrimps in the export value of marine products from the country is more than 70 per cent. Therefore, shrimp culture will be bringing in more of foreign exchange to the country.

Shrimp aquaculture and environmental preservation must be achieved as a unified motto for sustainable development.

If agricultural landless labourers and the local fishermen community are directly involved in shrimp culture, the entire benefits will be enjoyed by these grass root people. Some fishermen in the area have taken up shrimp farming and derived better benefits. Since profit rate is high, if the capitalists are allowed to capitalise the situation, inequalities in income and wealth will get accentuated. The start of shrimp farming and earning huge profit has resulted in clashes between the locals and the shrimp industrialists. Therefore the Government must protect the interests of the weaker sections with necessary legislations and also by implementing them effectively. Though shrimp farming is highly profitable, its polluting effects should not be undermined.

APPENDICES

Annexure–1
Shrimp Farming in India (2001–2002 To 2005–2006.)

Year	*Area under culture (ha)*	*Production (tons)*	*Productivity in (kg / ha)*
2001-02	172681	113660	658.21
2002-03	194040	127170	655.38
2003-04	186713	145770	780.72
2004-05	136393	125668	921.37
2005-06	184115	185990	1010.18

Source: MPEDA.

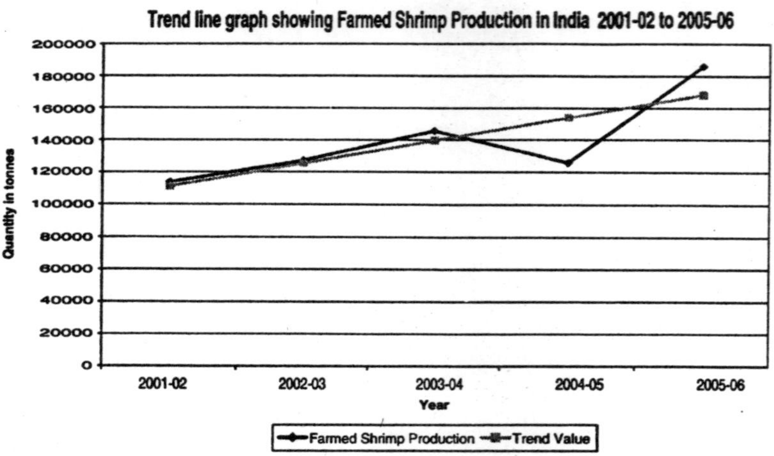

Annexure–2
Shrimp Farming in Tamilnadu

Year	*Area under culture (ha)*	*Production (tons)*	*Productivity in (kg/ha)*
2001-02	2596	3873	1491.91
2002-03	2650	4850	1830.19
2003-04	3800	5120	1347.37
2004-05	3684	6674	1811.62
2005-06	5451	7641	1401.76

Source: MPEDA.

Trend line graph showing Farmed Shrimp Production in Tamil Nadu 2001-02 to 2005-06

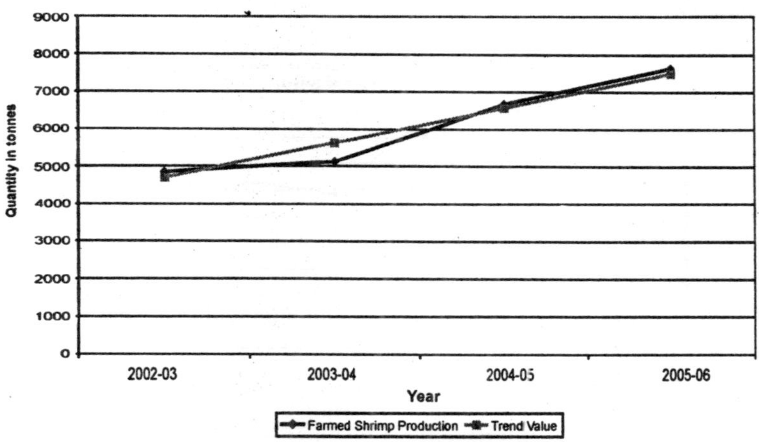

Annexure–3
Frozen Shrimp Exports from Chennai Port

Q → quantity in tonnes.
V → value Rs. In crores.

Year	*Quantity of Exports*	*Value of Exports*
2000-01	29752.01	1584.35
2001-02	35785.56	1498.75
2002-03	47046.36	1917.34
2003-04	34148.87	1385.83
2004-05	36631.52	1345.20
2005-06	32919.86	1248.95
2006-07	29366.95	1152.70

Source: MPEDA

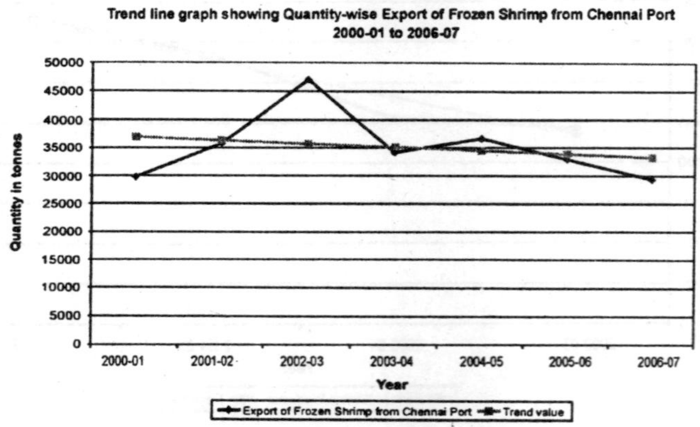

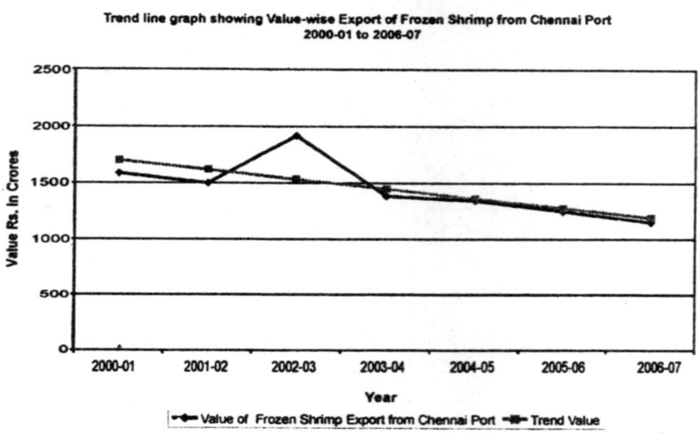

Annexure–4
Frozen Shrimp Exports from India (2000–2001 to 2007–2008)

Q → quantity in tonnes
V → value in tonnes

Year	*Quantity of Exports*	*Value of Exports*
2000-01	117508	4535.03
2001-02	121134	4100.37
2002-03	140831	4678.37
2003-04	129768	4013.07
2004-05	138085	4220.67
2005-06	145180	4271.51
2006-07	137397	4506.08
2007-08	135949	3931.95

Source: MPEDA.

Trend line graph showing Quantity-wise Export of Frozen Shrimp from India 2000-01 to 2006-07

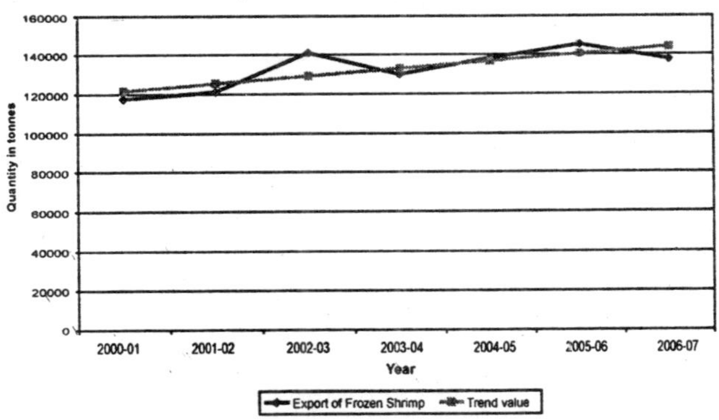

Trend line graph showing Value-wise Export of Frozen Shrimp from India 2000-01 to 2006-07

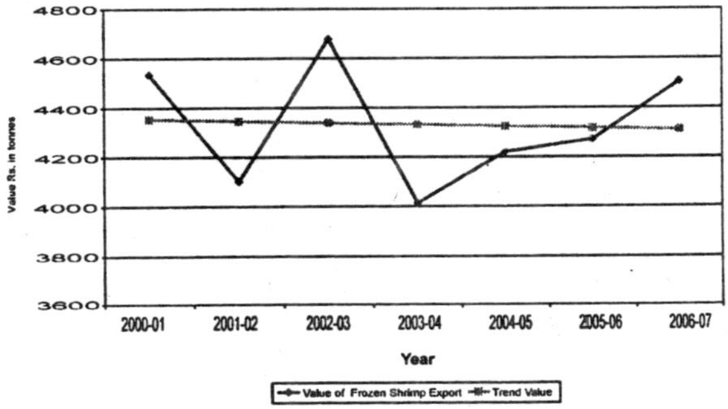

Annexure–5
Frozen Shrimp Exports From Tuticorin Port

Q → quantity in tonnes
V → value Rs. In crores

Year	*Quantity of Exports*	*Value of Exports*
2000-01	7600.38	378.48
2001-02	8231.96	356.11
2002-03	8605.20	335.38
2003-04	9565.69	357.40
2004-05	12864.15	455.37
2005-06	12508.49	454.50
2006-07	11814.08	456.74

Source: MPEDA.

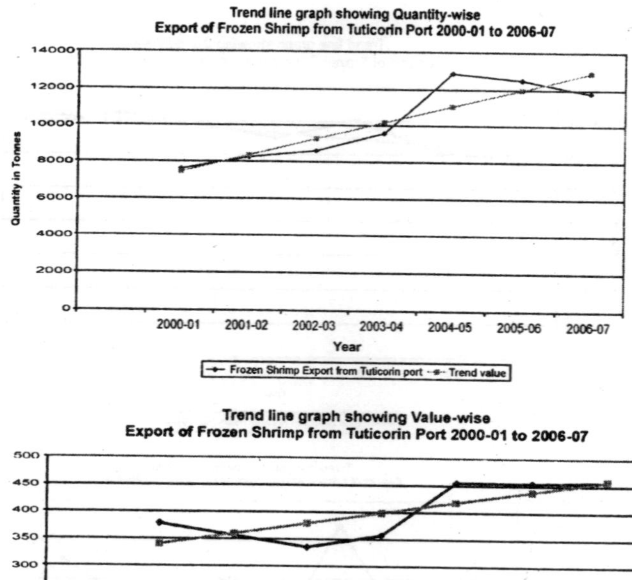

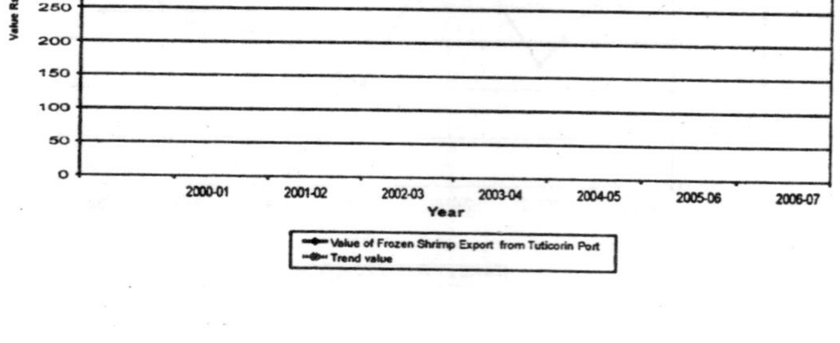

Annexure–6

Frozen Shrimp Exports from Tamilnadu (2000–2001 to 2006–2007)

Q → quantity in tonnes
V → Rs. in crores

Year	*Quantity*	*Value*
2000-01	37352.99	1962.83
2001-02	44017.52	1854.86
2002-03	55651.56	2252.72
2003-04	43714.56	1743.23
2004-05	49495.67	1800.57
2005-06	45428.35	1703.45
2006-07	41181.03	1609.44

Bar Diagram showing Quantity wise
Export of Frozen Shrimp from Tamil Nadu 2000-01 to 2006-07

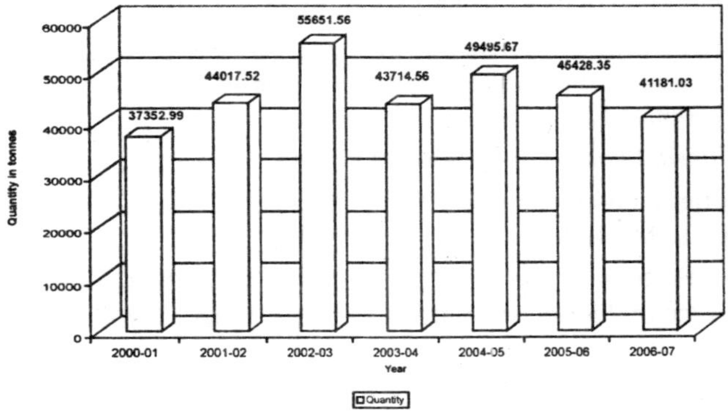

Bar Diagram showing Value–wise
Export of Frozen Shrimp from Tamil Nadu 2000-01 to 2006-07

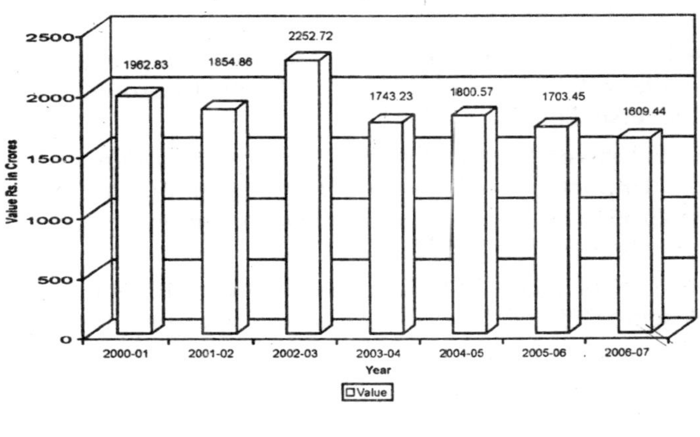

REFERENCES

Allen, D. (1991), "What are Transaction Costs?" Research in Law and Economics, 14, 1-18.

Akio Kanazawa (1995), "Seafood *News Letter*", Vol. 105, No. 3, April.

Anderson, Lee G. (1977), The Economics of Fisheries Management.

Ault, D.E. and G.L. Rutman (1989), "Land Scarcity, Economic Efficiency and African Common Law". Research in *Law and Economics* 12, 33-54.

Aqua International, Vol. 3, Sep. 1995, p. 6.

Banchong Tiensogrusmee (1995), "Seafood", *News Letter*, Vol. 105, No. 3, Apnl.

Christy, Francis T. and Scott, Anthony (1965), The Common Wealth in Ocean Fisheries, Baltimore: The John Hopkins University Press.

Banchong Tiensongrusmee. Environmental issues of shrimp forming South East Asian Experience. *Seafood News Letter*, Vol. 105, No. 3. p. 1-15 April 1995.

Dr. A. S. Bal (1995), "Seafood", *News Letter*, Vol. 105, No. 3, April.

Donnella, H. Meadows, Dennis L. Meadows, Jorgen Randers and William W. Bebens III (1972), The Limits to Growth (Newyork: Universe, Books), p. 23.

Dr. M. Sakthivel, President of AFI, The Research Paper Entitle on, the Impact of Aquaculture Development on the Coastal Environment, Presented at the Fourth National Symposium or Environment Held in Madras.

Gordon H. Scott (1954), " The Economic Theory of a Common Property Resource", *Journal of Political Economy*, 62, April, 124-142.

Griffin, Wade L, Lacewell, Ronald D and Nichols, John (1976), "Optimum Efforts and Rent Distribution in the Gulf of Mexico

Shrimp Fishery", *American Journal of Agricultural Economics,* 58, 644-52 .

HartWick, J. M (1980), 'Free Acces and the Dynamics of the Fishery': *Fishery. Bulletin* 77, 317-37 and D. F Spulber(eds); Essay in the Economics of Renewable Resources; Amsterdam, Newyork, Oxford: North-Hoiland.

Howe, C. (1979), Natural Resdurce Economics, Newyork; Wiley.

Jancy Gupta and K. Asoka Kumaran (19900, Unnithan-Scientific Prawn Culture in Home-steads-A Gainful Self Employment Opportunity for Coastal Women"-Marine Fisheries Information Services-at Nov. Dcc. Vol., No. 106 (CMRRl), Cochine, India.

John Kurien (1995), "The Hindu Survey of the Environment", Centre for Development Studies Thiruvananthanuram, pp. 43, Baltimore: The Johns Hopkins University Press.

Ibid, page 237.

Karunasagar and Indrani Karunasagar (1995), Shrimp Disease and Control Dept. of Fisheries, Microbiology, Mangalore.

K. B. Pillai (1995), "Souvenir Indaqua 95", Marine Products Export Development Authority, Cochin, p. 99.

K. Alagarswami (1995), Paper on, "Coastal Aquaculture Development and Environment Management", National Seminar held at Chennai on 1st Sep.

K. Alagarswarhy (1995), CIBA, "Seafood", *News Letter,* April, Vol. 105, No. 3, Madras.

Kelman, S. (1981), What Price Incentives?; Economists and Environment, West Port, Conn: Auburn House.

K. O. Isaac (1995), Aquaculture Pollution, much ADO About Nothing, Aqua International-August, Sept., pp. 10, Vol. 3, No. 4-5.

K.K.P. Panikkar (1993), "A Socio-Economic Analysis of Prawn Farming in Orissa State", Marine Fisheries Information Services", No. 126 (CMFRI) Cochin, p. 3-9

K. Raman & K. Gopinathan (1986), *"Journal Prawn Culture Central Inland",* Fisheries Research Institute, Madras, 11, pp. 55-58.

Krishnan M., Vasisht A. K. and Sharma B.M. (1991), Growth, "Geographical Distribution and Import Penetration of Shrimp Export from India", *Seafood Export Journal* Vol. XXI, No.10, Dec., pp. 5-13.

Ibid., pp. 7 & 8.

Krishnasrinath, A.M, Mohanan, K.P. Salini. Manual K. Sanhotra and A. Kanakkan (1994), "Marine Fisheries Information Services", No. 126 (CMFRl) Cochin, India. Jan., pp. 12 &13.

Lesser, J. and R. Zerbe (1995), "What can Economic Analysis Contribute to the Sustainability Debate?", Contemporary Economic Policy:' 13(13): 88-100.

Manual Sridhar (1994), "Technical and Economic Considerations for Shrimp Feed Production at South Chellanam, Ernakulam district, Part-II Field Trials and on F'arm Training on Feed Preparation". Marine Fisheries Information Services, Vol. 132, CMFRl, Sept., Cochin India. Pub. pp. 15-18

Murphy, G. I. (1977), 'Clupeids' in J.A Gulland, ed., Fish Population Dynamics(Newyork: Wiley)

P. V. Dehadrai (1995), "Stabilisation of Aquaculture Industry in India", Indaqua Exposition of Indian Aquaculture.

P. Vedavyasa Rao (1976), "Present Status of the Prawn Fishery of India", Today and Tomorrow's Publishers, New Delhi, p. 367 397.

Qasim (1997), National Aquaculture Week, Souvenir.

Rajalakshmi, N. (1999), Environment and Economic Development, Manak Publications, Pvt., Ltd.,

Rajalakshmi, N. (1999), Tamilnadu Economy, Business Link Corporation, Mumbai.

R. Sathiadas, K.K.P. Panikkar and A. Kanakkan (19942), Marine Fisheries Information Service", No. 126 (CMFRI) Cochin, India, Jan., pp. 12.

R. Kothandaraman (1994), "The Hindu Survey of Indian Industry, Spencer and Company Ltd., pp. 379.

Pearce, D. and R. Turner (1990), Economics of Natural Resources and the Environment; Baltimore, Johns Hopkins University Press.

Smith, V. L. (1968), 'Economics of Production from Natural Resource; *American Economic Review*, 58, 409-431.

Sutinen, Jon G. (1979), "Fishermen's Remuneration Systems and Implications for Fisheries Development", *Scottish Journal of Political Economy*, 26, 147-162.

Supreme Court of India (1996), Judgement in the Case Relating to Shrimp Farms.

Swaminathan, M. S. (1995), Prawn Culture Prone to disease, *Economic Times,*

Toman, M. (1994), "Economics and Sustalnability: Balancing Trade-Offs and Imperatives,· Land Economics. 70(4): 399-412.

T.V.R. Pillay (1992), Aquaculture and the Emironment", Fishing News Books, Osney head Oxford 0X2 OEL.

United Nations Development Programme, Human Development Report, 1993, Newyork: Oxford University Press, 1993.

Wilen, J. E. (1976), 'Common Property Resources and the Dynamics of Over-Exploitation: The Case of the North Pacificful Seal". Paper No. 3 in the Programme in Resource Economics; Department of Economics, University of British Columbia.

Zoeteweij, H. (1956), "Fishermen's Remuneration", In the Economics of Fisheries, eds. R. Turvey and J. Wiseman; Rome: FAO.

